An Introduction to
SOUTHERN
CALIFORNIA BIRDS

Herbert Clarke

Photographs by the Author

MOUNTAIN PRESS PUBLISHING COMPANY

Missoula, 1989

Library of Congress Cataloging-in-Publication Data

Clarke, Herbert.
    An introduction to southern California birds / Herbert Clarke.
        p.   cm.
    Bibliography: p.
    Includes index.
    ISBN 0-87842-233-1
    1. Birds—California, Southern.   2. Garden fauna—California
Southern.   I. Title.
QL684.C2C57   1989   89-30720
598.29794'9—dc19   CIP

Printed in Hong Kong by Mantec Production Company

Mountain Press Publishing Company
2016 Strand Avenue • P.O. Box 2399
Missoula, Montana 59806
(406) 728-1900

To my dearest Olga—the light of my life!

Acknowledgments

Birding in North America and overseas has been a consuming passion since I was a teenager. My favorite area continues to be southern California, because its varied habitats and mild climate give it tremendous potential for finding birds at any time of year. Many friends express the same ardor for this locality. Some of these birders contributed directly or indirectly to this book, and I am deeply grateful to them.

Several people stand out for their assistance. Kimball Garrett, whose knowledge of the status and distribution of southern California's birdlife is legendary, reviewed the text several times, making pertinent suggestions. Jonathan Alderfer, an outstanding bird artist, graciously drew and revised the map. Clyde Bergman, whose kindness and contagious enthusiasm made many arduous photographic expeditions delightful. Special thanks go to Ed Stern who led me through the intricacies of word processing. Jon Dunn, one of the world's leading birders, helped in the selection of the photographs. Joan Follendore advised on the composition of the text. The good judgement and fine contributions of my wife Olga, are apparent throughout the book.

I undertook photography of birds some thirty years ago, adding a new dimension to my interest in ornithology. This additional avocation has provided me with a constant challenge, and when successful, a full measure of satisfaction. Like every photographer, I have gone through the agony of missed or fumbled opportunities, and other times, the ecstasy of capturing my subject well on film. All pictures used in this book were taken by me, and the birds were photographed, in the wild, unrestrained.

Table of Contents

Southern California

The region covered by this book includes the eight southernmost counties of California: Santa Barbara, Ventura, Los Angeles, Orange, Riverside, San Diego, Imperial, and the southern half of San Bernardino County. This area has diverse natural bird habitats, with the human population concentrated on the western slopes of the mountains, and in the broad valleys along the Pacific coast.

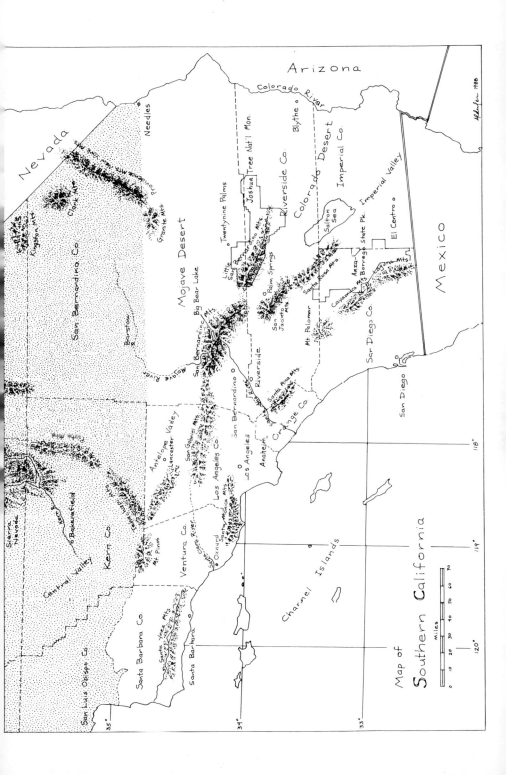

Map of
Southern California

Wrentit at leaking faucet

Introduction

The purpose of this book is to enhance enjoyment of southern California living by introducing readers to the intriguing world of bird study. It's not necessary to make detailed notes on observations, delve deeply into taxonomy, or any other tedious and time consuming activity, in order to indulge this pleasure. My aim is to help you learn about, and enjoy, wild birds for their own sake, without engendering a mental reservation to observe them in an orderly or scientific manner. This is not a comprehensive field guide, but most likely encountered species are illustrated. Accompanying paragraphs give interesting facts about the life histories of those birds pictured.

Attracting Birds

An effective way to attract birds to home gardens, is to supply a suitable water source, protected from cats, along with planting for cover. The water could be anything from a drip of some kind, such as a slow running, or leaky faucet, to an elaborate birdbath. Always, water should be regularly changed to keep it clean. Foods that lure birds include chicken scratch, bread crumbs, peanut butter, raisins, apples, suet, and sunflower seeds. Again, these diet supplements should be kept clean, sheltered from weather, and protected from cats. Landscaping with fruiting and berry-bearing trees and shrubs is another excellent way to keep birds coming. Your local nursery can give advice as to which plants are best suited to your area. Water, food, and sugar-water feeders attract many feathered visitors, allowing them to constantly delight and entertain you for very little cost and effort. Various commercial bird feeders are available, but a suitable homemade one may suffice. Generally, birds do not make use of bird houses or boxes in southern California

American Robin in bird bath

Identifying Birds

In order to simplify naming the species one finds in southern California, this book is divided into areas where specific birds are generally seen—mountains, deserts, and so forth. Bear in mind, that since man has placed many types of plants and trees in unnatural settings, and water where before there was none, birds often appear in unexpected places. Availability of fresh water greatly affects avian distribution. This liquid is of such importance that most birds will travel out of their normal habitats, and overcome natural shyness, to drink and bathe. Further, with the region's uneven topography, which includes elevations ranging from below sea level (Salton Sea), to over 11,000 feet (San Bernardino Mountains), in close proximity, there is considerable movement, influenced by season, weather, and food supply.

Overall lengths are shown in inches, and measured from bill tips to tail tips. This can be misleading, especially in species with long bills such as thrashers, hummingbirds, or shorebirds. Even a small size variation is exaggerated by type of build (stocky or slender). Remember this when attempting to identify similar appearing birds. Also, plumage often changes with season, gender, and age. When appropriate, these differences are indicated in the text. Songs and calls are difficult to describe; words convey only a general impression of vocalization. Keeping this fact in mind helps when listening to a bird.

When first you don't succeed in locating the illustration of the subject under observation, look through other chapters, because it may be pictured in another habitat. Then, if not successful, you should consult a field guide to help in identification. Please understand not every naturally occurring species—approximately 500 in southern California—is depicted in this book.

General Information

Many birds of foreign origin appear in the wild in southern California. These include various species of parrots, ducks, and unfamiliar types such as flamingos, peafowl, and finches. Some probably escaped from captivity during transit through the region, or while being kept as pets, and others were deliberately introduced. They survive because of the mild climate and easily obtain-

4

able food. Most of these exotic birds, with a few exceptions, are not discussed here.

All birds have two names—an English name and a scientific one. The latter is used when referring to species throughout the scientific and non-English speaking world. Names used and arrangement are taken from the accepted reference, American Ornithologists Union's *Check-List of North American Birds*, sixth edition, 1983.

Should you wish to learn more about birds, there are ways to gain knowledge and skill in identification. A good binocular is of great help in perceiving subtle differences in plumage. Buy the highest quality you can afford. Your local camera store or specialized optical source can suggest which kind of binocular is best for your needs and purse. References at the end of the book give you information sources to further your study. A helpful organization you can join is your local Audubon Society or similar nature group.

There are many ways to watch birds. Individual interest and skill vary widely. It's a personal decision how deeply one wants to become involved in this fascinating endeavor. At whatever level you desire to participate, relax, forget your cares and enjoy.

Hooded Oriole at hummingbird feeder

Chaparral, Los Angeles County

Birds Included in Chapter 1

Sharp-shinned Hawk
Red-tailed Hawk
California Quail
Rock Dove
Spotted Dove
Common Barn-Owl
Great Horned Owl
Black-chinned Hummingbird
Anna's Hummingbird
Nuttall's Woodpecker
Acorn Woodpecker
Downy Woodpecker
Northern Flicker
Western Flycatcher
Scrub Jay
Plain Titmouse
Bushtit
House Wren
Ruby-crowned Kinglet
Hermit Thrush
American Robin

Wrentit
Northern Mockingbird
California Thrasher
Cedar Waxwing
Warbling Vireo
Orange-crowned Warbler
Yellow Warbler
Yellow-rumped Warbler
Black-headed Grosbeak
Rufous-sided Towhee
Brown Towhee
White-crowned Sparrow
Hooded Oriole
Northern Oriole
Golden-crowned Sparrow
House Finch
Lesser Goldfinch
Brewer's Blackbird
House Sparrow
American Crow

Chapter 1

Birds of the Western Slopes
and Coastal Valleys

Included in this chapter are those portions of southern California, from the edges of the montane forests on the western slopes of the coastal mountains, generally about the 5,000-foot level, through the lower foothills and broad valleys, down to the Pacific coast. This is the most densely populated region of southern California, containing ninety percent of the human population, but it also has the most diverse natural habitats. Birdlife has been greatly affected by man's alteration of the environment. In the built-up urban areas of cities such as Los Angeles and San Diego, certain species have prospered (House Finches and Northern Mockingbirds, for example), while others have declined or disappeared. Sometimes, depending on food and weather, desert and mountain birds appear, seasonally, in gardens and parks here. Also, large numbers of birds migrate through the area in spring and fall, on their way to northern nesting grounds or southerly wintering grounds.

Most widespread of the various habitats in this region is chaparral, a dense, thick-leaved, dwarf forest. It ranges from the edge of the mountains' coniferous forest down to sea level, and averages fifteen to twenty-five inches of rainfall each year. Fires, as devastating as they appear, are a natural phenomenon, actually helping maintain the health of the vegetation by natural pruning, and permitting new growth to prosper. Chaparral is not continuous, but is interspersed with other habitats—open grassy areas, oak and streamside woodlands. Also, there are pockets of unique micro-habitats tucked away in lesser known localities, where birds with specialized requirements can regularly be found. Unfortunately, as many parts of southern California become increasingly urbanized, these natural treasures are being overrun and eliminated forever.

7

Sharp-shinned Hawk · *Accipiter striatus* · 12"

As with most hawks, the females are distinctly larger than the males. Immatures are brown and streaked, differing from adults. In winter and during migration, these small hawks are fairly common over much of southern California. Sharp-shinned Hawks prey mainly on small birds, and are one of three similar, low-flying woodland hawks that occur in southern California. All are characterized by short, rounded wings, and long tails for speed and agility.

Red-tailed Hawk · *Buteo jamaicensis* · 22",wingspread 50"

A common, large hawk frequently seen perched in trees and on tops of poles, or soaring slowly overhead in a wide variety of locations, ranging from freeway edges and residential areas, to high mountains and low deserts. The chunky, broad-winged, short-tailed shape is distinctive, and the reddish tail identifies the adult. The immature Red-tailed Hawk has a banded tail, lacking the adult's color. Food consists primarily of small rodents, snakes, rabbits and insects. This hawk builds a large, bulky nest, high in a tree or on a cliff face.

California Quail · *Callipepla californica* · 10"

This is the state bird of California, and is found in brushy foothills, usually near a water source. Female plumage is more subdued than the male's. The nest is well hidden in vegetation on the ground, and contains a large clutch of eggs, usually twelve or more. This helps offset the high mortality rate of the eggs and young, due to predation by snakes, cats, rats and other animals. Soon after the nesting season, the adults of several families gather with their young, and travel together in coveys. Quails are seed eaters, and can easily be attracted to the garden by a regular supply of bird seed or chicken scratch. Most frequently heard call is a loud *chicago*.

Sharp-shinned Hawk - adult

Red-tailed hawks - pair at nest

California Quail - male

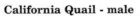

Rock Dove *Columba livia* 12 1/2"

The Rock Dove is the familiar park pigeon of urban areas. This bird was probably the first species to be domesticated, and through the centuries, a wide variety of plumage patterns and colors, from white to dark purple, resulted. The wild variety looks like the photograph. These doves originated in Europe and Asia. Rocky hillsides—the normal habitat—have been replaced in southern California by buildings, ocean cliffs and caves.

Spotted Dove *Streptopelia chinensis* 12"

Another dove introduced from Asia is the Spotted Dove. This species' numbers have remained relatively stable for the last fifty years. Commonly found in parks and residential areas of southern California, it's particularly fond of foreign plantings of eucalyptus, pines, citrus and other trees. Immatures lack spotted collars, but their rounded tails distinguish them from Mourning doves which have pointed tails.

Common Barn-Owl *Tyto alba* 16"

Barn-Owls have declined with the development of southern California. They can still be found in some urban sections, but are more common in rural areas. Nesting sites are sheltered places such as buildings, barns (hence the name) and other man-made structures, as well as trees (especially palms), caves, and similar places. Most people are unaware of their presence because these owls are strictly nocturnal, roosting in dark, secluded locations during daylight hours. When observed at night, they appear to be huge white moths, flying silently, ghostlike on long, broad wings. Barn-Owls are very beneficial to man, feeding primarily on rodents.

Rock Dove

Spotted Dove

Common Barn-Owl

Great Horned Owl   *Bubo virginianus* 22"

The "horns" are really feather tufts. These owls are widespread, found in both woodlands and suburban areas. They begin nesting early in the year, and make their presence known by their deep, resonant hoots. Later in the season, their newly-fledged young are heard at night, begging for food, in blood-curdling, raspy screams. Great Horned Owls are the largest of North American owls, and can often be seen perched, or in flight, at dusk or dawn. Other birds noisily harass these owls whenever they're discovered during daytime by their avian tormentors.

Black-chinned Hummingbird

Archilochus alexandri 3 3/4"

A violet band at the lower edge of his black throat, on males only, is often difficult to see. Females so closely resemble other small hummingbird females that it's almost impossible to differentiate them. Nests, made from various plant fibers are unadorned, and have the facility to stretch as the two young grow. Black-chinned Hummingbirds are resident from late March to August, wintering in Mexico. They are most common in oak and streamside woodlands, and can easily be attracted by feeders.

Great Horned Owl

Black-chinned Hummingbird - male

**Black-chinned Hummingbird -
female feeding young in nest**

Anna's Hummingbird   *Calypte anna*   4"

The most common, all-year resident hummingbird, of southern California, is Anna's Hummingbird. This species is often confused with the Ruby-throated Hummingbird of eastern North America. Unlike his eastern relative, the brilliant rose-red of the male Anna's extends over his head like a hood. This color, as in most hummingbirds, can only be seen in good light, and at other times appears black. Female Anna's closely resemble several other species of female hummingbirds, but are slightly larger and dingier gray below.

Nuttall's Woodpecker   *Picoides nuttallii*   7 1/2"

Like many woodpeckers, the male and female are similar in plumage, except the male has a patch of red on his head. Woodpeckers have thick-walled skulls which, combined with sharp, chisel-like bills and long-barbed tongues, enable them to drill and probe for insects in the bark of trees. The male's loud drumming on a resonant tree limb, or even a utility pole, helps establish his territory. The Nuttall's Woodpecker commonly nests in chaparral and streamside woodlands.

Acorn Woodpecker   *Melanerpes formicivorus*   9"

Appropriately named, these are woodpeckers of pure oak woodlands, or mixed forests where oaks are prevalent. These birds embed acorns in tree trunks or wooden utility poles, for future consumption. Females look like males, except for having black patches separating white foreheads from red crowns. In flight, the white rump and wing patches are distinctive. Acorn Woodpeckers are sociable and gather in noisy colonies, making loud, parrot-like calls.

Anna's Hummingbird - male   **Nuttall's Woodpecker - male**

Acorn Woodpecker - male

Downy Woodpecker

Picoides pubescens 6 3/4"

The white backs of these woodpeckers separate them from the equally common and similar Nuttall's. Lowland forests, parklands and residential areas are Downy Woodpeckers' preferred habitats. They do not migrate, and can be found year-round in southern California. Woodpeckers excavate new holes in trees, every nesting season, while the previous years' holes are often used by other birds such as starlings, bluebirds, or small owls.

Northern Flicker

Colaptes auratus 12 1/2"

Like many woodpeckers, flickers have conspicuous white rumps, which combined with the undulating flight pattern and distinctive red flight feathers, readily identifies this species. Female Northern Flickers lack the red moustache marks of the males. In addition to the usual woodpecker food of insects, flickers feed on berries, fruit, and routinely probe on the ground for ants. These birds are found from treeline down to sea level. In addition to trees, they often perch and drum on utility poles, and sometimes become a nuisance when they drill into wooden buildings.

Western Flycatcher

Empidonax difficilis 5 1/2"

The Western Flycatcher looks much like other small flycatchers which have pale eye rings and two whitish wing bars. Care should be taken when attempting to identify these species, as even experts have difficulty in distinguishing some of them. Yellowish underparts, combined with the tear-drop shape of the eye ring, make this flycatcher easy to identify. Western Flycatchers are commonly found March to September, in open woodlands, usually near streams.

Downy Woodpecker - male **Northern Flicker - male**

Western Flycatcher

Scrub Jay *Aphelocoma coerulescens* 11 1/2"

Often incorrectly called "Blue Jay" (which is a crested jay of eastern North America), the Scrub Jay is a conspicuous member of the crow family, and is found throughout the year, not only in residential areas, but in brushy areas and chaparral, from sea level up to the edge of mountain coniferous forests. It is noisy and aggressive, and frequently will devour the eggs and young of smaller birds. This jay can be tamed and will take food, such as peanuts, from the hand.

Plain Titmouse *Parus inornatus* 5 3/4"

These are our smallest birds with crests, and are found in open, mixed woodlands. Titmice are year-round residents, nesting in old woodpecker holes or other tree cavities. They feed on insects, seeds and fruit, and will come to bird-feeding trays. Natural acrobats, they often cling upside-down to tree limbs, while foraging for food. Plumages of the sexes are alike. Their song, heard chiefly in spring, is a whistled *weety weety weety*.

Bushtit *Psaltriparus minimus* 4 1/2"

Males have black eyes instead of the yellow of females. Bushtits build long, beautifully woven nests, suspended from trees or bushes. After the nesting season they gather in large flocks, hurriedly moving about in a seemingly random manner, constantly evoking soft, twittering notes. Several Bushtits may bathe together, in a small pool of water such as a bird bath. They do not migrate, and can be seen in southern California at any time of year, especially in chaparral and other brushy and wooded areas.

Scrub Jay

Plain Titmouse

Bushtit - female

House Wren   *Troglodytes aedon*   4 3/4"

These diminutive wrens continuously burst forth with loud, lilting songs, especially during nesting season. Strictly insect eaters, House Wrens are found throughout North and South America. They are most common in residential areas, and woodlands with a brushy understory, building their nests in all kinds of small, natural and man-made cavities. Males and females look alike and frequently return each breeding season to territories where they previously nested.

Ruby-crowned Kinglet   *Regulus calendula*   4 1/4"

The male's ruby-colored crowns are visible only when these tiny birds become excited. Kinglets nest in local and northern coniferous forests and in winter, move to lower elevations of the foothills and valleys. Peanut butter, along with sugar water of hummingbird feeders are attractions to them. The normal diet of kinglets consists mainly of insects, obtained by foraging in trees, thickets and brush. The song, heard in the spring and fall, is a remarkably loud, long, varied warble of high and low notes.

Hermit Thrush   *Catharus guttatus*   6 3/4"

Distinctive reddish tails identify these thrushes. Large numbers winter in southern California, but Hermit Thrushes are somewhat shy and not readily observed, although they are attracted to birdbaths. They nest further north, in the mountains, where they're noted for their beautiful flute-like songs. Food consists of berries and insects, consumed near, or on, the ground. Sexes appear alike and are not separable in the field.

House Wren

Ruby-crowned Kinglet

Hermit Thrush

American Robin
Turdus migratorius 10"

Common throughout the region, robins nest from high mountain forests to lowland suburban parks and gardens. In wintertime, birds that nest at higher elevations move to lower elevations, even to the deserts. A familiar sight, Robins run over lawns searching for earthworms—their favorite food. They are also fond of various berries. Spotted breasts of the young show their relationship to the thrush family. A clutch of four, unmarked bright-blue eggs, is laid, from which the term "robin's egg blue" is derived. Females are slightly paler than males.

Wrentit
Chamaea fasciata 6 1/2"

The habitat of this bird is exclusively chaparral. The song is a loud, metallic trill, reminding one of a bouncing ping-pong ball. The Wrentit often cocks its long tail, much like a wren, but is not a member of the wren family. Shy and usually remaining hidden in thick brush, it feeds on insects and berries, but can be attracted to gardens by water drips and peanut butter. Sexes look alike and stay together for life in small, restricted areas.

American Robin - male

American Robin - fledgling

Wrentit

Northern Mockingbird   *Mimus polyglottos*   10"

The exuberant song of mockingbirds, loudly ringing out, day and night, from a tall perch is a delight to most people, but a nuisance to some. Mockingbirds are expert mimics of other birds, and also imitate barking dogs, squeaking wheels, whistles and many other loud sounds. They are easily attracted to gardens by water and food, such as raisins, bread and plantings of berry bushes. Mockingbirds nest, year-round, throughout southern California, in towns, cities, deserts and farmlands, wherever there are scattered trees and shrubs. The flashing white wing patches and white outer-tail feathers, combined with their joyous songs, make mockingbirds welcome residents to many communities.

California Thrasher   *Toxostoma redivivum*   12"

This is a bird of the lowland chaparral and streamside woodland thickets. Mockingbirds and thrashers are members of the same family and have similar songs, but thrasher's calls are much more subdued. The distinctive long, down-curved bill is used to rake fallen leaves and probe the ground for grubs, spiders and seeds. It can be attracted to gardens by bird seed and crumbs. Like Mockingbirds, sexes are alike.

Cedar Waxwing   *Bombycilla cedrorum*   7 1/4"

Cedar Waxwings are a familiar winter sight in southern California. Smooth plumage and waxlike, red tips, on the secondaries of their wings, give this species its unusual name. Gathering in flocks by the hundred, waxwings will gorge themselves on berries. While feeding or flying, they continuously call with a soft, high-pitched trill. These birds nest in southern Canada and northern United States.

Northern Mockingbird

California Thrasher

Cedar Waxwing

Warbling Vireo

Vireo gilvus   5 1/2"

Typical of most species of vireos, these are dull-colored, little birds, which move deliberately through the foliage of trees, in open, deciduous woodlands. They are common, but usually overlooked, because of these characteristics. Nests are well made cups, woven of fine grass and suspended from forks of branches. Their song consists of several melodious, warbling phrases continually repeated. Warbling Vireos winter in Central America.

Orange-crowned Warbler

Vermivora celata   5"

In many areas of southern California, especially chaparral, these plain-appearing warblers are common throughout the year. The orange crowns are usually concealed by olive head feathers. These little birds are constantly active, searching on lower tree limbs, and in brush, for insects. Nests are built on the ground at bases of bushes or low in shrubs. Occasionally, they can be attracted to gardens by peanut butter or dripping water.

Warbling Vireo

Orange-crowned Warbler

**Orange-crowned Warbler -
bathing and showing orange crown**

Yellow Warbler   *Dendroica petechia* 5"

The female lacks the conspicuous reddish streaks of the male. This bird breeds during the summer in moist, wooded habitats, but during migration, can be found almost anywhere. The Yellow Warbler's range is the greatest of all wood warblers, nesting across the continent, from northern Canada to Mexico, and wintering from Mexico to northern South America. Like other species of small, yellow birds, it's often incorrectly called "Wild Canary."

Yellow-rumped Warbler   *Dendroica coronata* 5 1/2"

This appropriately-named warbler displays its conspicuous yellow rump in all seasons and plumages. It nests in coniferous woodlands from Alaska to the mountains of southern California, moving south, and down into lower elevations, in the fall. Most of the year, the Yellow-rumped Warbler looks rather drab except for the rump. Then in early spring, the male attains his beautiful breeding plumage. You may find this bird listed in older books as Audubon's Warbler.

Yellow Warbler - male

Yellow-rumped Warbler - spring male

Yellow-rumped Warbler - fall female

Black-headed Grosbeak
Pheucticus melanocephalus 8 1/4"

The massive bill is used to crack open seeds and nuts, which are the staples of this grosbeak's diet. It also feeds on insects and berries, and can easily be attracted to bird feeders with chicken scratch. A summer resident of open woodlands, at most elevations, the Black-headed Grosbeak winters in Mexico. Singing a fast series of loud warbles, the grosbeak's song is similar to the robin's, but livelier.

Rufous-sided Towhee   *Pipilo erythrophthalmus* 8 1/2"

Not quite as common as Brown Towhees, but similar in habits, Rufous-sided Towhees scratch on the ground with both feet, searching for seeds, insects and berries. Females are slightly duller than males, but have the same colors and pattern. Concealed nests are constructed by females, on the ground or low in dense brush. These birds come to gardens and feeders readily. Their song is a drawn-out, buzzy *chweeee*.

Black-headed Grosbeak - male

Black-headed Grosbeak - female

Rufous-sided Towhee

Brown Towhee
Pipilo fuscus 8 1/2"

These common birds are tame and prominent, especially in chaparral and suburban gardens. Nests are bulky and built in the densest part of bushes or trees. Habitually feeding on the ground, consuming seeds and insects, they are easily attracted to gardens by peanut butter, bird seed and chicken scratch. A rapid series of sharp notes on one pitch, ending in a trill, is the typical song. These towhees are non-migratory, and plumages of the sexes are alike.

White-crowned Sparrow
Zonotrichia leucophrys 7"

An abundant winter resident, White-crowned Sparrows are found in a variety of habitats from brushy fields to open woodlands. Their high-pitched, plaintive songs are emitted even in non-nesting seasons. As with most sparrows, white-crowns are primarily seed eaters, and are easily attracted to gardens. They nest from the mountains of southern California north, and along the coast from central California to Alaska.

Brown Towhee

White-crowned Sparrow - adult

White-crowned sparrow - immature

Hooded Oriole

Icterus cucullatus   8"

Hooded Orioles prefer to nest in palm trees, using shredded fibers of the leaves to construct their nests. They are extremely fond of sugar-water in hummingbird feeders but their normal diet is nectar obtained from various flowering plants, along with insects found in blossoms. These birds are summer residents, with the bulk of the population migrating to Mexico for the winter. Females resemble female Northern Orioles, except the bellies of Hoodeds are yellowish, and they have longer, more curved bills. Young males have the black throat of older adult males, but otherwise resemble females. Their call is a rising, whistled *wheet*.

Northern Oriole

Icterus galbula   8 3/4"

These orioles spend most of the year in Mexico and Central America, returning in spring to nest in open woodlands of southern California. They are common in suburban gardens where they're easily attracted by the sweetened water in hummingbird feeders. Their song is a loud, flute-like warble. Plumages of the sexes are quite different, as shown in the photographs. Young males look like females, but have some black on their throat. Older books refer to this species as Bullock's Orioles.

Hooded Oriole - male

Northern Oriole - male

Northern Oriole - female

Golden-crowned Sparrow *Zonotrichia atricapilla* 7"

Immatures and winter adults lack the heavy black band over the eye, and have less intense gold on the crown. These sparrows are winter visitors, found usually in brushy areas. In the spring, adults attain their breeding plumage, just before returning to nesting sites in western Canada and Alaska. Primarily seed eaters, Golden-crowned Sparrows come to feeding stations for bread crumbs, peanut butter and grain.

House Finch *Carpodacus mexicanus* 6"

The plumage of adult males ranges from bright red to orange. Females and young males are quite different, with no red or orange, but basically brown with brown streaks on the underparts. House Finches are common from lower mountain elevations to sea level, in arid scrub, chaparral, open woodlands and urban areas. Being finches, they feed mostly on seeds, but will also eat fruit. These attractive birds have a loud, melodius song. Nests are built in a wide variety of locations—tree cavities, buildings, shrubs, vines, cactus and old bird nests. House Finch nests have an unclean appearance, because the parents do not carry off the waste of the nestlings as do other species.

Golden-crowned Sparrow - breeding adult

House Finch - male

House Finch - female

Lesser Goldfinch
Carduelis psaltria 4 1/2"

The smallest of North American goldfinches are strictly seed eaters. They build their nests in dense brush or in the thick foliage of trees, such as sycamores or cottonwoods, usually near water. After the nesting season, Lesser Goldfinches gather in flocks, to feed in weedy fields and open woodlands. Distinctive white patches on the wings are conspicuous, especially when flying. Males have a long, exuberant, high-pitched song which is vocalized in flight, or when perched on the top of a tall tree.

Brewer's Blackbird
Euphagus cyanocephalus 9"

These blackbirds gather in large flocks, and range from the seashore up into mountain meadows, usually near water. Often with other species of blackbirds, they forage on the ground for insects and seeds, in towns as well as in agricultural communities. Females are gray-brown with brown eyes, and young birds resemble females. Nests are a mixture of mud and grass, lined with fine materials and built in bushes or trees, often around human habitations. Brewer's Blackbirds are comonly found in appropriate habitats year-round.

Lesser Goldfinch - male

Lesser Goldfinch - female

Brewer's Blackbird - male

House Sparrow

Passer domesticus   6 1/4"

The black bibs of the males are obscured by gray feather tips in the winter. Formerly known as English Sparrows, House Sparrows have spread over much of North America, since their introduction from Great Britain, in the middle of the Nineteenth Century. They are year-round residents, almost always near man. Nests are constructed of grass, paper, feathers and a variety of other materials, usually placed in nooks and crannies of buildings, but an individual might build a round, dome-shaped nest in a tree or shrub. House Sparrows are gregarious and aggressive, and can drive off much larger birds from feeding or nesting sites. They eat a wide variety of food, including seeds, berries, insects and even garbage. Sometimes considered a pest because of their large, noisy flocks, these sparrows brighten otherwise drab areas of southern California cities where they may be the only birdlife in evidence.

American Crow

Corvus brachyrhynchos   17 1/2"

Another species benefiting by the urbanization of southern California are crows. Like most members of the family, they are considered intelligent, because their flocks seem to be somewhat organized. Crows are wary, but quite common in suburban areas, as well as in open woods of rural regions. Aggressive and not restricted in what they eat, crows consume just about anything edible. Similar in appearance to ravens, but smaller, crows do not soar as much, and are more likely to be seen in lowland, wooded habitats. Individuals have a variety of calls with their most common being *caw* frequently mixed with imitations of various sounds. Plumages of the sexes are alike.

House Sparrow - male

House Sparrow - female

American Crow

San Bernardino Mountains, San Bernardino County

Birds Included in Chapter II

Mountain Quail
Band-tailed Pigeon
Spotted Owl
Calliope Hummingbird
Rufous Hummingbird
Red-breasted Sapsucker
Williamson's Sapsucker
White-headed Woodpecker
Violet-green Swallow
Western Wood-Pewee
Steller's Jay
Pinyon Jay
Clark's Nutcracker
Red-breasted Nuthatch
White-breasted Nuthatch
Pygmy Nuthatch
Canyon Wren
American Dipper

Western Bluebird
Mountain Bluebird
Townsend's Solitaire
Nashville Warbler
Black-throated Gray Warbler
Townsend's Warbler
MacGillivray's Warbler
Wilson's Warbler
Western Tanager
Mountain Chickadee
Green-tailed Towhee
Chipping Sparrow
Fox Sparrow
Dark-eyed Junco
Purple Finch
Cassin's finch
Pine Siskin
Lawrence's Goldfinch

Chapter II

Mountain Birds

Wildlife communities covered in this chapter range from above the 5,000 foot elevation. Included are the dry, east-facing slopes, and on west-facing slopes, coniferous forests with annual precipitation of about fifty inches. Extremes of temperature result in a much shorter growing season than in lower elevations. Freezing weather and covering snow can often render sustenance unattainable to birds. As a consequence, bird movement is more pronounced, and largely affected by the availability of water and food.

Provisions provided by people, can greatly influence the number of birds around homes in any season. Feeding, once started, should be continued on a frequent and regular basis, because the possibility of a sudden, extreme change in weather at these higher elevations can be disastrous to birds that have become dependent on human support.

As in other areas of southern California, habitats in the mountains are diverse. Coniferous forests, meadows, lakes, streamside deciduous woodlands and even elements of the desert are in close proximity, and interspersed with human development.

Mountain Quail   *Oreortyx pictus*   11"

Thin, long, head plumes distinguish these beautiful birds from the other two species of California quails. Sexes look alike, except for the females' shorter head plumes. Like the others, Mountain Quails are fond of seed and come to feeders. They live in dense mountain brush and edges of coniferous forests. Nests are well concealed, slight depressions, scratched out in the ground at bases of bushes, rocks or logs. In winter, these quails descend to lower elevations, usually in large coveys.

Band-tailed Pigeon   *Columba fasciata*   14 1/2"

These are the most common, wild pigeons of the mountains. Superficially they resemble the abundant, introduced pigeon of suburban areas, but are distinguished by yellow bills with black tips, and the pale band at the end of their tails. Young birds lack white napes and iridescent areas found on the necks of adults. Band-tailed pigeons wander in flocks, in search of acorns—their favorite food—and are seen increasingly at lower elevations, in parks and suburban gardens. They're easily attracted to bird seed feeders.

Spotted Owl   *Strix occidentalis*   17 1/2"

Spotted Owl's numbers have been greatly reduced by indiscriminate shooting and habitat destruction. Residing in dense woodlands, they're usually strictly nocturnal. On occasion, in the daytime, an individual can be seen perched in an exposed location. Because they're trusting, these large owls can be closely approached and are vulnerable to harm. Their call resembles the barking of a dog, and food, like most owls, consists primarily of rodents and insects.

Mountain Quail

Band-tailed Pigeon   **Spotted Owl**

Calliope Hummingbird
Stellula calliope   3 1/4"

A summer resident of the mountains, it's the smallest North American bird. The male's gorget is composed of colored rays, or streaks, rather than the solid pattern of other hummingbirds. Typical of hummingbirds, after mating, the female alone builds the nest, incubates two eggs, and rears the young. Most adult males depart for wintering grounds in Mexico by mid-July, with females and immature males leaving later.

Rufous Hummingbird
Selasphorus rufus   3 3/4"

Nesting from Alaska to the northwestern United States, Rufous Hummingbirds migrate in large numbers through southern California. They generally travel by way of the foothills and mountains, to and from wintering grounds in southern Mexico. The adult male makes a characteristic trilling sound in flight, and his conspicuous all-rufous appearance distinguishes him from other hummingbirds. Females and immatures have varying amounts of reddish-brown and green in their plumage.

Calliope Hummingbird - male

Rufous Hummingbird - male

Rufous Hummingbird - female

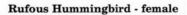

Red-breasted Sapsucker   *Sphyrapicus ruber*   8 1/2"

This member of the Woodpecker Family is common in coniferous and mixed coniferous-deciduous forests of mountain ranges. Sapsuckers drill small horizontal rows of holes in the bark of trees, feeding on sap, and insects, especially ants, attracted to the sap. Nests usually are dug in live deciduous trees near water and lined with wood chips. Unlike many woodpeckers, plumages of the sexes are alike in this species.

Williamson's Sapsucker   *Sphyrapicus thyroideus*   9"

When Williamson's Sapsuckers were first described, the male and female were thought to be separate species because they look so different from each other. Usually found in dry, higher elevation coniferous forests, a few move south or to lower elevations in winter. Nests are holes drilled in trunks, or dead tops, of partly decayed pines or firs, from five to sixty feet above ground. Their diet is the same as other sapsuckers.

Red-breasted Sapsucker

Williamson's Sapsucker - male   Williamson's Sapsucker - female

White-headed Woodpecker *Picoides albolarvatus*   9 1/4"

The only woodpecker with a white head found in southern California, is the appropriately named White-headed Woodpecker. The female is shown. Males have a red patch on the nape, and young birds have some red on the forecrown as seen in the picture. These age and sex differences are typical of most woodpeckers. This species feeds primarily on pine cone seeds, with the addition of insects gleaned from loose tree bark.

Violet-green Swallow *Tachycineta thalassina*   5 1/4"

An abundant resident in foothill and mountain open woodlands, the Violet-green Swallow nests in old woodpecker holes and natural cavities in trees and cliffs. It often forms a loose colony with other individuals of the species. White flank patches extending onto the sides of the rump are the primary, identifying field marks. The female is duller than the male, and young are gray-brown above. Swallows, unlike most birds, migrate during daylight hours, catching insects on the wing, as they travel.

Western Wood-Pewee *Contopus sordidulus*   6 1/4"

Wood-Pewees are common summer residents of open woodlands. In typical flycatcher fashion, they sally forth from an exposed perch, catch their insect prey in mid-air, and often return to the same perch. Wood-Pewees winter from southern Mexico to South America, migrating through most of southern California, to their breeding grounds in mountains and foothills. Their call is a short, slurred *peeer*.

White-headed Woodpecker   **Violet-green Swallow**

Western Wood-Pewee

Steller's Jay
Cyanocitta stelleri 11 1/2"

Bold and aggressive, Steller's Jays are the western counterpart of the eastern Blue Jays. They often scavenge at campgrounds and picnic areas, and will invade mountain garden seed feeders. In spite of their boldness, these handsome jays are shy and secretive near their nests—usually high in dense tree foliage. Calls are strident and raucous, mixed with whistles and gurgling notes, along with hawk-like screams.

Pinyon Jay
Gymnorhinus cyanocephalus 10 1/2"

The Pinyon Jay looks like a small blue crow, walking, hopping and flying similarly to crows. This is an unusual bird in that it's more gregarious and nomadic than other jays, with flocks wandering through a wide range of habitats, depending on the availability of food. It generally prefers arid, pinyon-juniper hillsides and the dry, yellow pine woodlands at higher altitudes. Like most members of the Crow Family, sexes look alike.

Clark's Nutcracker
Nucifraga columbiana 12"

This member of the Crow Family is normally found in high elevation coniferous forests. White wing patches and white outer-tail feathers, combined with deep, slow wing beats, easily identify the species. Like other members of the family, it's a bold scavenger at campgrounds and picnic areas. After nesting, this nutcracker sometimes moves down into the deserts and other lowland areas of southern California.

Steller's Jay

Pinyon Jay

Clark's Nutcracker

Red-breasted Nuthatch   *Sitta canadensis*   4 1/2"

Red-breasted Nuthatches are acrobatic, constantly foraging on tree trunks and limbs, for conifer seeds and insects. Primarily a bird of high mountain coniferous forests, some years, their numbers increase dramatically, and individuals or small groups are found in many habitats, at any elevation. These birds nest in cavities they've excavated in stubs, or branches, of dead trees, and smear pitch of coniferous trees around the entrances.

White-breasted Nuthatch   *Sitta carolinensis*   5 3/4"

This species is found in a wider variety of habitats than other nuthatches, and is common in deciduous lowland forests, as well as coniferous forests at higher elevations. They're as comfortable foraging for insects, head down on tree trunks, as head up. This attribute enables White-breasted Nuthatches to find food other species, which glean only upward, may miss. These birds frequently come to feeding stations for seeds and suet.

Pygmy Nuthatch   *Sitta pygmaea*   4 1/4"

These small nuthatches gather in loose flocks, emitting soft, peeping notes, while searching for insects and pine seeds among clusters of pine needles at ends of branches. Pygmy Nuthatches reside mainly in yellow pine forests and have little seasonal movement. Pairs dig nesting holes, lining them with pinecone scales and plant down, in dead trees or fallen logs. Sexes are outwardly alike.

Red-breasted Nuthatch

White-breasted Nuthatch

Pygmy Nuthatch

Canyon Wren   *Catherpes mexicanus*   5 3/4"

Here we have a most beautiful wren, in both appearance and song. The Canyon Wren's preferred habitats are deep, shady canyons, and cliffs near water. It creeps, mouselike, among loose rocks and in crevices, searching for insects and spiders. Occasionally it nests in buildings. This bird is non-migratory, and is heard more often than seen. Its loud, liquid song is a series of descending notes and, when reverberating off canyon walls, evokes an ethereal feeling.

American Dipper   *Cinclus mexicanus*   7 1/2"

With specialized adaptations—extra plumage insulation, a movable flap over its nostrils, protective extra eyelids, strong legs and toes, and short, stubby wings—this unusual bird actually moves through water as easily as through air. The American Dipper, or "Water Ouzel" as it's often called, is found along clear, rushing, mountain streams, at all seasons. It feeds almost entirely on aquatic insects. The large, bulky nest, constructed wholly by the female, is placed on rocky ledges near streams, or behind waterfalls. A habit of constantly bobbing while hopping on streamside rocks is thought to be responsible for the name "Dipper."

Western Bluebird   *Sialia mexicana*   7"

Chestnut breasts and backs distinguish these common bluebirds from their close relatives, Mountain Bluebirds. Western Bluebirds are found in open woodlands, at most altitudes, and move to lower elevations in the winter. They nest in old woodpecker holes and other cavities in trees and poles. The females and young are not as brightly colored as the males. In addition to the usual fare of insects, bluebirds are fond of berries and fruit.

Canyon Wren

American Dipper

Western Bluebird - male

Mountain Bluebird
Sialia currucoides 7 1/4"

Mountain meadows and other open areas, at elevations above 5,000-feet, are the habitats of these totally blue birds. Insects are caught on the wing, or by hovering low over the ground and dropping down on them. Mountain Bluebirds build nests in natural cavities or man-made structures, and after the breeding season, they gather in flocks and move to lower elevations. Females and young are much duller than the males, appearing gray-brown with only a tinge of blue.

Townsend's Solitaire
Myadestes townsendi 8 1/2"

The solitaire is appropriately named for its retiring nature, and that it's usually seen singly or in pairs. This member of the thrush family is fairly common in the high coniferous forests, and its nest is placed on the ground, partially concealed under an overhanging bank or bush. Solitaires have buff wing patches, and white outer-tail feathers, especially obvious in flight. The plain appearance of this species is more than compensated for by its beautiful song, consisting of a prolonged series of rapidly warbled, loud, clear notes, sung from the top of a tall tree or in flight.

Nashville Warbler
Vermivora ruficapilla 4 3/4"

Warblers are the butterflies of the bird world, actively flitting high in the trees and down to the ground, in pursuit of insects. The Nashville Warbler was named after the city where it was first described in the early Nineteenth Century. Breeding across southern Canada and northern United States, only a few nest in our local mountains. Plumages of the sexes are similar except the female is duller than the male. This species migrates throughout southern California, to and from its wintering grounds in Mexico and Guatemala.

Mountain Bluebird - male

Townsend's Solitaire

Nashville Warbler - male

Black-throated Gray Warbler
Dendroica nigrescens 5"

This warbler favors the dry oak and coniferous mountain woodland of southern Canada and western United States. Plumages of the sexes are similar, except some of the black of the male is replaced by white and gray in the female. As with most warblers, this species is generally seen only during migration, with a few individuals occasionally overwintering in southern California. Its song is a buzzy, high-pitched *weezee weezee weezee zeet.*

Townsend's Warbler   *Dendroica townsendi* 5"

Residents of northwest coniferous forests, Townsend's Warblers migrate in the spring throughout southern California, but primarily via the mountains during fall. Most spend the winter in Central America, but a few remain in our region. Like many warblers, plumage patterns of the sexes are similar, with the females being duller, and fall immatures resembling females. Food consists of insects and spiders, actively gleaned from bushes and trees.

MacGillivray's Warbler   *Oporornis tolmiei* 5 1/4"

Unlike most warblers, MacGillivray's inhabit moist, dense undergrowth, and nest on, or low to, the ground. They are fairly common, but seldom seen because of their retiring habits. Like many western warblers, this species' nesting areas are in mountains, with their wintering range south of the United States. During migration, they're found in areas as diverse as deserts, coastal lowlands and foothills.

Black-throated Gray Warbler - male

Townsend's Warbler - male

MacGillivray's Warbler - male

Wilson's Warbler
Wilsonia pusilla   4 3/4"

The black cap of the male is either reduced or missing altogether in the female. This is an oft-seen bird, especially during migration. The Wilson's Warbler nests in low, dense thickets, usually near water. Formerly it bred from lowlands to the mountains, but, due mainly to cowbird parasitism, breeding populations of lower elevations were greatly reduced. Individuals occasionally remain in coastal southern California through winter.

Western Tanager
Piranga ludoviciana   7 1/4"

Tanagers are perhaps our most beautiful birds. The large tanager sub-family contains many colorful species (about 242), mainly found in the tropics of Central and South America, with only a few reaching North America. Western Tanagers are birds of the coniferous forest in the summer, migrating to Mexico and Costa Rica in fall. Food consists primarily of insects and berries,but they can be attracted to bird feeders by dried fruit, oranges, and cake. Plumages of the sexes are quite different, as illustrated.

Wilson's Warbler - male

Western Tanager - male

Western Tanager - female

Mountain Chickadee

Parus gambeli   5 1/4"

A delight to watch, these friendly little birds can be enticed to feed from the hand, at campgrounds and picnic areas. A frequent call is a hoarse *chick-adee-adee*. Nests are often located in natural cavities, and after the breeding season, chickadees occasionally wander to lowland, open woodlands and riparian thickets. Frequently, they will join other birds in loose feeding flocks, searching for insects, spiders and seeds.

Green-tailed Towhee

Pipilo chlorurus   7 1/4"

Both sexes look alike and are colorful members of the sparrow family, but difficult to see in low, dense, mountain chaparral, and brushy meadows. However, in spring, males will sing from an exposed perch. The song consists of a pleasant series of clear notes followed by a coarse trill, similar to the Fox Sparrow's. The Green-tailed Towhee scratches on the ground like other towhees, searching for seeds, berries and insects, and goes to feeders containing bread, birdseed and grain. The wintering range is mainly in Mexico, but a few remain in the southern California lowlands.

Chipping Sparrow

Spizella passerina   5 1/2"

The breeding adult is illustrated. Males and females look alike, and after the nesting season, their chestnut caps are replaced by streaked crowns. These birds are common residents of open, montane forests where they make their presence known by singing a long, even-pitched, buzzy trill. Chipping Sparrows feed on seeds and insects, and regularly go to feeding stations. Gathering in flocks, they wander to lower elevations in fall and winter.

64

Mountain Chickadee

Green-tailed Towhee

Chipping Sparrow

Fox Sparrow *Passerella iliaca* 7"

Our largest sparrow has feeding, nesting habits, and song much like the Green-tailed Towhee. The bird illustrated is our summer mountain resident. In winter and migration, at lower elevations, additional Fox-Sparrows come to southern California from other parts of North America. These visitors vary in color, ranging from dark brown to rufous and gray, all still retaining the basic Fox Sparrow plumage pattern.

Dark-eyed Junco *Junco hyemalis* 6 1/4"

This member of the sparrow family was called Oregon Junco, until various races, with dark eyes, found in other parts of the country, were determined to be all one species. In southern California, the Dark-eyed Junco is a summer resident of conifer, and mixed conifer-deciduous forests in the mountains. After nesting, it moves to the lowlands and is joined by other juncos from further north and east. The female is brownish-gray overall, and she alone, builds the nest, incubates the eggs, and often has two broods a season. The song is like the Chipping Sparrow's, but slower and more musical.

Purple Finch *Carpodacus purpureus* 6"

One of the three red finches of southern California, this species breeds in oak and oak-conifer woodlands at middle elevations. The basic color of the Purple Finch male is actually rose-red, whereas the female is brown and heavily streaked, greatly resembling female House Finches and Cassin's Finches. In winter, some move into foothills, lowlands and deserts. There's a great increase in numbers during so-called "flight years."

66

Fox Sparrow

Dark-eyed Junco - male

Purple Finch - male

Cassin's Finch
Carpodacus cassinii 6 1/4"

Cassin's Finches are residents at higher elevations, although there's considerable overlap among the three red finches. Male Cassins' have bright crimson caps, and little streaking, but females closely resemble female House Finches and Purple Finches. Food consists of seeds, buds, insects and berries. Males sing from treetop perches or in flight, loud, warbled songs that combine qualities of other finches' songs, but are more varied.

Pine Siskin
Carduelis pinus 5"

The streaked, brown, plumage usually conceals the yellow tail base and central flight feathers, except in flight. Pine Siskins nest in pine woodlands, and travel in flocks. They forage in trees or on the ground for seeds and insects. In winter, they're found throughout the foothills and lowlands of southern California, with numbers at any one time and place, varying greatly. Their most distinctive and frequent call is a rising, high-pitched, buzzy trill.

Lawrence's Goldfinch
Carduelis lawrencei 4 3/4"

The erratic movements of the Lawrence's Goldfinch make it hard to predict its location at any certain time. This is our least common, but most beautiful, goldfinch. Its nest, a neat cup of wool, grasses and feathers, is constructed in a variety of habitats, including riparian thickets, open coniferous forests and chaparral, in loose colonies. The female lacks the black patches that are conspicuous on the male's face and chin.

Cassin's Finch - male

Pine Siskin

Lawrence's Goldfinch - male

Colorado Desert, Riverside County

Birds Included in Chapter III

Gambel's Quail
White-winged Dove
Greater Roadrunner
Western Screech-Owl
Costa's Hummingbird
Common Poorwill
Ladder-backed Woodpecker
Gila Woodpecker
Vermilion Flycatcher
Ash-throated Flycatcher
Common Raven

Verdin
Cactus Wren
Rock Wren
Blue-gray Gnatcatcher
Phainopepla
Le Conte's Thrasher
Abert's Towhee
Brewer's Sparrow
Black-throated Sparrow
Scott's Oriole

Chapter III

Desert Birds

The term "desert" often conjures images of infinite views of lifeless sand and rock. But, in southeastern California, deserts are alive with plants and animals uniquely adapted to this special environment. Rainfall averages less than ten inches a year, and temperature variance can be extreme in a relatively short period. Frequent winds blow, with gusts sometimes reaching hurricane velocities. Elevations range from below sea level, near the Salton Sea, to over 5,000 feet on eastern slopes of mountains.

Southern California deserts are not uniform in their composition of plant life. This, in turn, influences the number and variety of birds observed. Some examples of arid communities are sagebrush scrub, pinyon-juniper woodland, Joshua tree woodland, and creosote bush scrub. Interspersion of these various habitats is determined by elevation, weather, and soil conditions. As rugged as the desert appears, it is, in fact, a fragile ecosystem where thoughtless desecration can leave permanent scars on the landscape.

In spite of these difficult conditions, resident species are able to thrive on available food which supplies nutrition and required moisture. Most birds migrating in the west, travel through deserts, southeasterly and northwesterly, depending on time of year. They find enough food and water to continue their arduous journey between northern nesting sites and sub-tropical or tropical wintering grounds.

Here in the deserts, as in most southern California regions, there has been considerable development. Extensive crop irrigation, artificial lakes, and watering of suburban parks and homes, created oases that allow many species to flourish—birds which otherwise would be scarce or nonexistent in this habitat.

Gambel's Quail *Callipepla gambelii* 11"

This species is similar in habits and appearance to the California Quail, but the Gambel's Quail is paler and has chestnut sides. It's a bird of arid scrublands and thickets, usually near a water source. The nest is a hollow, scraped in the ground, in tall grass or at the base of a bush, lined with grasses, sticks and feathers. After nesting, adults and young gather in large coveys to forage for food and water. Being a seed eater, as are other quails, this species frequently goes to feeders.

White-winged Dove *Zenaida asiatica* 12"

Large white wing patches, conspicuous in flight, easily separate these doves from the more common Mourning Doves. White-winged Doves are normally birds of the hot, dry interior, but a few wander to the coast in fall and winter. They feed on grain, seeds, and cactus fruit. Nests are built in dense foliage of trees, with previous years' nests of other birds sometimes utilized. Their call is a low-pitched *who-cooks-for-you*.

Greater Roadrunner *Geococcyx californianus* 23"

A year-round resident, the roadrunner is a symbol of the desert, although found in chaparral as well. This member of the Cuckoo Family can fly, but seems to prefer running. It nests low in thickets or clumps of cactus, with young hatching in order of laying, so it's possible to have, in the same nest, new hatchlings and fledglings almost ready to leave. Food includes lizards, snakes, insects, rodents and berries.

Gambel's Quail - male, front; female, rear

White-winged Dove

Greater Roadrunner

Western Screech-Owl
Otus kennicottii   8 1/2"

Screech-Owls have prominent "ear" tufts which they often flatten, as shown in the photograph. Although common, they are strictly nocturnal, and not easily seen. These are wide-ranging owls, found in many habitats, including deserts and woodlands. Nesting is in natural cavities and old woodpecker holes. Their food consists of rodents, insects and small birds. The call is not a screech, but a series of evenly pitched whistles that start slowly, increasing into a whinny.

Costa's Hummingbird
Calypte costae   3 1/2"

The male's violet hood and elongated gorget separate him from other hummingbird males. The female appears much like other female hummingbirds, but her nest is distinctively decorated with spider webs, feathers and lichens. This species is resident in the desert and dry chaparral, and winters mainly in northwestern Mexico, with a few remaining in southern California all year. Its diet consists of nectar, and insects found in flowers or on plants.

Western Screech-Owl

Costa's Hummingbird - male

Costa's Hummingbird - female

Common Poorwill   *Phalaenoptilus nuttallii*   7 3/4"

The name poorwill is taken from its most common call. A nocturnal bird, it spends the day roosting under a shrub or in grass, feeding at night by leaping from the ground to catch an insect in air, returning to the same or nearby spot. Excellent camouflage protects the incubating parent in its nest, a bare scrape in the ground, partly shaded by a bush, but sometimes completely exposed. This bird is also found in dry woodlands and chaparral.

Gila Woodpecker   *Melanerpes uropygialis*   9 1/4"

Pronounced "heela," Gila Woodpeckers are named after the Gila River in Arizona where the species was first discovered. Found only in the extreme southeastern corner of this state, near the Colorado River, they are resident in groves of cottonwoods, date palms and plantings of shade trees. Females lack the red caps of the males, and both sexes show conspicuous white wing patches in flight.

Ladder-backed Woodpecker   *Picoides scalaris*   7 1/4"

This is the desert version of the Nuttall's Woodpecker of the western foothills. The two similar species are best identified by range and habitat, with Ladder-backeds favoring cactus and other low-growing plants of the eastern, dry areas, while Nuttall's inhabit the more moist chaparral, scrub oak and wooded canyons. Ladder-backed Woodpeckers forage in small trees and shrubs for insect larvae, and on the ground for ants.

Common Poorwill

Gila Woodpecker - male

Ladder-backed Woodpecker - male

Vermilion Flycatcher   *Pyrocephalus rubinus*   6"

This striking flycatcher's range extends south all the way to Argentina. In California, it's found in desert oases, usually near water, and in the winter, occasionally is seen near the coast. The female looks quite different—brown above and streaked below, and has a salmon-colored belly. In the spring, the male puts on a spectacular mating display, with feathers puffed and wings vibrating, it hovers butterfly-like before the female.

Ash-throated Flycatcher   *Myiarchus cinerascens*   8 1/2"

Like many flycatchers, the Ash-throated has a characteristically large, somewhat crested, head. This species is more colorful than other flycatchers, with its yellowish underparts, and reddish coloration in the tail. Breeding habitats are varied, ranging from low deserts to high coniferous forests. The nest is usually built in a natural tree cavity, rarely more than twenty feet above ground. Most winter south, in Central America.

Common Raven   *Corvus corax*   24"

Often confused with crows, ravens are larger and have wedge-shaped tails, rather than the rounded ones of crows. Voices are also quite different. Ravens make croaking, gurgling calls and notes. Both sexes look alike, except females are somewhat smaller. These birds are scavengers, and their diet consists of a wide variety of plant and animal food. Ravens soar like hawks, ranging over arid and semi-arid habitats, high in mountains, and down into lower elevation residential areas.

Vermilion Flycatcher - male

Ash-throated Flycatcher

Common Raven

Verdin   *Auriparus flaviceps*   4 1/2"

The ball-shaped nests of Verdins are common sights in mesquite and other dense, thorny shrubs of the desert. Frequently, similar roosting or wintering nests are also built. These are sprightly little birds, actively flitting and emitting soft chip-like notes, as they search for insects and berries. Verdins do not require open water, but rely on food for their primary source of moisture. Males and females appear similar, and are year-round residents.

Cactus Wren   *Campylorhynchus brunneicapillus*   8 1/2"

Our largest wrens build nests like Verdins except bigger. In addition to constructing sites for raising young, they, too, build nests for roosting. Cactus Wrens can move rapidly through spiny cactus and shrubs, with impunity. Food includes insects, berries and an occasional lizard or tree frog. They sometimes visit bird feeders for bread and raw apples. Their song, a typical sound of the desert, can be heard most times of the year, and consists of low, even-pitched series of harsh notes.

Rock Wren   *Salpinctes obsoletus*   6"

These birds are fairly common residents of arid, rocky slopes and washes. Nests are hidden in abandoned rodent burrows, loose rocks, and other natural crevices, and are made of grasses, rootlets and weed stems, lined with fur, horsehair and feathers. Food consists of insects and spiders, found abundantly about bare rocks. Rock Wrens are not confined to deserts, but may be found in suitable localities along the coast, on the Channel Islands and in the foothills.

Verdin

Cactus Wren

Rock Wren

Blue-gray Gnatcatcher   *Polioptila caerulea*   4 1/2"

The Blue-gray Gnatcatcher is one of two common gnatcatchers found in arid habitats, with this one also frequenting chaparral and woodlands. The other species is the Black-tailed Gnatcatcher. Habits and appearances are similar in the two birds. The main difference is that the undertail of the Blue-gray is white, and that of the Black-tailed is mostly black. Also, the Black- tailed breeding male has a black cap which the Blue-gray lacks. Both gnatcatchers are very fidgety, constantly twitching their tails, while actively searching for insects in low shrubs and trees.

Phainopepla   *Phainopepla nitens*   7 3/4"

Silky Flycatcher is an appropriate name for the Family which includes the Phainopepla. The male displays white wing patches in its floppy flight. The female's and young bird's wing patches are gray. Besides insects, another favored food of the Phainopepla is mistletoe berries. The presence of a previous year's nest is often indicated by a clump of mistletoe, in a tree or shrub, growing from the seeds excreted by the nestlings. In addition to the desert, this bird nests in chaparral and oak woodlands, where often two broods a season are raised.

Blue-gray Gnatcatcher - male

Phainopepla - male

Phainopepla - female

Le Conte's Thrasher
Toxostoma lecontei 11"

The Le Conte's Thrasher is the palest of several species of thrashers found in southern California. It prefers dry, sparsely vegetated washes and slopes, and has the habit of running rapidly with its black tail cocked up. This thrasher hides its large, bulky nest in dense shrub, usually on the edge of a wash. In spring, the male sings from a low bush, his loud, rich song, in early morning, again in the cool evening, and sometimes after dark.

Abert's Towhee
Pipilo aberti 9 1/2"

These towhees are desert equivalents of Brown Towhees of coastal slopes and valleys. Abert's Towhees resemble Brown Towhees in general appearance and actions, but have distinctive black faces, and are shyer than their more confiding cousins. Seed feeders attract both species to home gardens. This bird occurs in scrub, orchards and tree thickets. Pairs mate for life, and there is no sexual plumage difference.

Brewer's Sparrow
Spizella breweri 5 1/2"

In spring and summer, this is a bird of the desert at various elevations, especially where sagebrush abounds. In winter, it travels into brushy and scrubby growth of arid, lower elevations. The Brewer's Sparrow is generally overlooked, because it's a shy, little, brown bird. Sometimes, it will come to a feeder, and become fairly tame. The long, varied, insect-like song is a distinctive sound of sagebrush country.

Le Conte's Thrasher

Abert's Towhee

Brewer's Sparrow

Black-throated Sparrow *Amphispiza bilineata* 5 1/2"

Formerly called Desert Sparrow, the Black-throated Sparrow is truly a bird of the desert. It's independent of water, obtaining moisture requirements from seeds and insects gleaned from the ground. The open nest is concealed in dense, low bushes and shrubs. Plumages of the sexes are the same, but young birds lack the black on the throat, and are finely streaked below and on the back. This sparrow does not migrate long distances, but there is considerable movement throughout our region, in fall and winter.

Scott's Oriole *Icterus parisorum* 9"

The bright, lemon-yellow color of the male makes him a singular feature of the high desert savannas. His song, a mixture of rich whistled notes, can be heard virtually all day, from dawn to dusk. The nest is an intricately woven cup, suspended from the ends of leaves of yuccas or Joshua trees. Wintering grounds are in Mexico, with a few individuals remaining in desert canyons throughout the year.

Black-throated Sparrow

Scott's Oriole - male

Scott's Oriole - female

Oak Savanna, Santa Barbara County

Birds Included in Chapter IV

Cattle Egret
Turkey Vulture
Black-shouldered Kite
Northern Harrier
Golden Eagle
American Kestrel
Prairie Falcon
Mountain Plover
Sandhill Crane
Mourning Dove
Burrowing Owl
Short-eared Owl
Lesser Nighthawk

Say's Phoebe
Western Kingbird
Horned Lark
Cliff Swallow
Yellow-Billed Magpie
Water Pipit
Blue Grosbeak
Loggerhead Shrike
European Starling
Lark Sparrow
Savannah Sparrow
Western Meadowlark
Brown-headed Cowbird

Chapter IV

Birds of Agricultural Areas, Grasslands, and Savannas

Perhaps the habitats most severely altered by man's activities are these open areas. Extensive agricultural pursuits such as farming and grazing, have all but eliminated natural vegetation. This, in turn, has reduced the number of species normally found here. However, some birds have prospered, in spite of seeming adversity. Among these are American Kestrel, Cattle Egret, and Cliff Swallow—all welcome beneficiaries. Not-so-welcome are starlings, cowbirds, and other blackbirds which gather in large flocks in fall and winter. These aggressive species often drive away song birds, attack crops, and create a nuisance with their droppings.

Savannas—grasslands with scattered trees such as oaks—have suffered greatly from overgrazing of cattle and sheep. What little underbrush that did exist has been cleared, eliminating food and cover for birds, as well as protection for young trees. This has resulted in once beautiful sections of rolling hills, dotted with magnificent trees, being gradually converted into sterile, bare rangeland or housing tracts.

But in many orchards and other farm areas, it's still possible to observe interesting birds, and to attract them to gardens. There are species which are adaptable and opportunistic, so that by proper planting, and making water available, the country home can be brightened by the presence of nature's feathered jewels.

Cattle Egret
Bubulcus ibis 20"

Originally Cattle Egrets associated with herds of wild animals, primarily in Africa, and ate insects stirred up by animal movement. These egrets' numbers vastly increased when they learned to follow domestic livestock. They invaded South America, late in the Nineteenth Century, then moved north through Central America, reaching the United States around 1950, and have since spread wherever there is extensive cattle or farming activity. Cattle Egrets are colonial, whether feeding in fields or nesting in partially drowned trees. During the breeding season both sexes display orange-buff plumes on their necks, backs and crowns, all of which are absent at other times of the year, when they become entirely white, except for yellow bills and legs.

Turkey Vulture
Cathartes aura 27", wingspread 69"

Named after the bare, red skin of the adult's head—resembling a turkey's head—vultures perform a valuable service in removing carrion and other refuse from the countryside. Their digestive systems destroy whatever disease germs are present. They have excellent eyesight and are among the few birds with well-developed smell senses. Large flocks can be seen soaring on thermals, with motionless wings, in search of food or migrating. Vultures do not build nests, but lay their eggs on sheltered ledges, in caves or hollow logs, and sometimes in abandoned buildings. They are common transients in spring and fall, but rare summer and winter residents.

Black-shouldered Kite
Elanus caeruleus 16" wingspread 42"

Formerly called White-tailed Kite, this beautiful bird of prey has benefited by man's agricultural activities. The Black-shouldered Kite is found throughout the world in its favored habitats, grasslands, fields, marshes and roadside borders. It hunts by hovering, with wings rapidly flapping, then plunging on its prey of field mice and insects. Wintering groups of these birds often roost together in clumps of large trees in marshy bottomlands.

90

Cattle Egret - breeding adult with young

Turkey Vulture

Black-shouldered Kite

Northern Harrier *Circus cyaneus* 20", wingspread 43"

Conspicuous white rumps identify these hawks of marshes and fields. Females are larger, and brown above, where males are gray. When hunting for rodents, snakes, insects and frogs, they course back and forth, low to the ground, but fly higher during migration and courtship. Northern Harriers roost and nest on the ground, but numbers are down because of the diminution of marshland habitat. This species is called Marsh Hawk in most older literature.

Golden Eagle *Aquila chrysaetos* 35", wingspread 84"

These magnificent, and much maligned, eagles are found all over the Northern Hemisphere. They have been falsely accused of wantonly destroying livestock and even of carrying off human babies. Golden Eagles have been poisoned, shot and hunted down from airplanes, in addition to suffering from habitat destruction and detrimental effects of pesticides. Despite this constant persecution, they're still frequently seen in open country of southern California, from lower elevations to higher montane regions, nesting on cliff ledges or in trees. Food consists primarily of small animals, snakes, birds, carrion, and only rarely will these eagles attack healthy, larger animals. Only adults have a golden cast on the backs of their heads and necks. Younger birds display varying amounts of white in the wings and tail.

American Kestrel *Falco sparverius* 10 1/2", wingspread 23"

Male kestrels have blue-gray wings and all-russet tails, with only one broad, dark band at the tip. This species is the smallest, most common falcon in southern California. These are birds of open country and suburban areas, nesting in holes of trees, niches in buildings, and on cliffs. Kestrels regularly alight on prominent perches and utility wires to watch for prey on the ground. They hunt insects, rodents, small snakes and birds, often by hovering much like Black-shouldered Kites.

Northern Harrier

Golden Eagle - immature

American Kestrel - female

Prairie Falcon   *Falco mexicanus*   18", wingspread 39"

Prairie Falcons are birds of prey, able to fly rapidly with long, pointed wings. Most prominent field marks are dark areas where wings join the body on the underside. Numbers have declined because of frequent illegal capture for falconry, and poisoning from pesticides ingested from their diet of rodents and birds. Plumages of sexes are alike, with females being larger, a common trait of falcons. Nests are placed on protected cliff ledges, sometimes in old raven or hawk nests.

Mountain Plover   *Charadrius montanus*   9"

Plovers are generally considered shorebirds, but this species is a bird of dry plains, grasslands and plowed fields. Mountain Plovers nest in high plateaus of the Rocky Mountain and Plains States, and spend winter in southern California from about mid-October to the end of February. They often gather in flocks of hundreds, with their protective coloration making them almost invisible.

Sandhill Crane   *Grus canadensis*   41"

Here is another wintertime bird of southern California. Large flocks of these stately cranes feed during daytime in expansive dry fields, retiring to areas of shallow water at night. Cranes differ from herons and egrets by flying with their long necks extended. Adult plumage, the same in both sexes, is reached in about three years, with immatures being brown of various shades, and having no red on their crowns. Food is varied, and includes grain, berries, snakes, insects, rodents and small birds. Nesting is in Alaska and northern Canada, south to northern California.

Prairie Falcon

Mountain Plover

Sandhill Crane

Mourning Dove
Zenaida macroura   12"

Mourning Doves are the most abundant and widespread doves of our area. Habitats include agricultural areas, deserts, cities and open forests of most elevations. The name comes from their "mournful" cooing; and their wings make whistling sounds in flight. These are slender birds with long, pointed tails. They're extremely fond of birdseed at feeding stations. Nesting occurs every month of the year in southern California.

Burrowing Owl
Athene cunicularia   9 1/2"

This long-legged owl is active both day and night. A resident of open country, it can be seen standing on fence posts or on dirt embankments of roadsides, in golf courses, and at the edge of fields. Burrows in the ground are dug or enlarged for nests. Food includes insects, rodents, lizards and frogs. The Burrowing Owl's flight is low and undulating, with occasional hovering. In winter, summer residents of our area are joined by migrants from the north.

Short-eared Owl
Asio flammeus   15"

Short-eared Owls are winter visitors to grasslands and weedy fields of southern California. They're often seen hunting at dawn or dusk, erratically low flying, or sitting on exposed perches or the ground, ready to pounce on their unwary prey of mice, insects and small birds. Somewhat gregarious, numbers of Short-eared Owls will hunt together over the same field, especially where small rodents are abundant. These owls have been recorded on every continent except Australia.

Mourning Dove

Burrowing Owl

Short-eared Owl

Lesser Nighthawk　　*Chordeiles acutipennis*　8 1/2"

Here are birds that are most active at dusk and dawn, flying fairly low, with a fluttery motion, catching insects on the wing. Adults show a distinctive white or buff bar near the wing tips. Nighthawks are not hawks, but are members of the Nightjar Family, as are Poorwills (Desert Chapter). Eggs are placed on the bare ground, and are incubated only by females. These nighthawks are commonly seen over dry fields and areas of scrubby growth. The call is a rapid, vibrating trill.

Say's Phoebe　　*Sayornis saya*　7 1/2"

Say's Phoebes are year-round residents of arid, open country, with numbers augmented in winter from outside the region. In typical flycatcher fashion, these birds dart from perches on bushes, rocks, or posts to catch flying insects. Often, when perched, they fan and dip their tails nervously. Nests are built on rocky shelves, in natural tree cavities or protected niches of buildings. A typical call is a plaintive *pee-ee*.

Western Kingbird　　*Tyrannus verticalis*　8 3/4"

This species is a common, summer resident of open country with scattered trees. It perches on wires, fences or other exposed sites, and acts in the usual manner of flycatchers—darting out to catch insects on the wing. Western Kingbirds will aggressively attack hawks, crows, and ravens. The usual call is a sharp *whit*, sometimes rapidly repeated. Sexes appear alike. They winter from Mexico south to Nicaragua.

Lesser Nighthawk - female on eggs

Say's Phoebe - pair at nest

Western Kingbird

Horned Lark
Eremophila alpestris 7 1/4"

So-called "horns" of this abundant species are merely tufts of feathers. Males go through elaborate courtship displays, flying and circling at considerable heights, while voicing high-pitched, tinkling songs. Nests are built on the ground, sometimes exposed, but often near clumps of grass or clods of earth. After nesting, Horned Larks gather in large flocks, moving across bare fields, feeding on insects, weed seeds and waste grain. These birds walk or run, rather than hop. Black tails with white outer feathers are conspicuous field marks.

Cliff Swallow
Hirundo pyrrhonota 5 1/2"

This is the swallow of San Juan Capistrano fame, and although its migration schedule is quite regular, it's not as precise as legend tells. The natural site of the gourd-shaped Cliff Swallow nest is on cliff faces, but this bird has readily adopted man-made structures, such as beneath bridges, eaves of buildings or any convenient vertical surface. It's a colonial nester, gathering with other swallows, all excitedly fluttering their wings, to collect mud from the ground for nests. Enormous quantities of harmful bugs are consumed, entirely on the wing.

Yellow-billed Magpie
Pica nuttalli 16 1/2"

Yellow-billed Magpies are endemic to California, found only in the Sacramento Valley and coastal valleys south to Santa Barbara County, and nowhere else in the world. Magpies are gregarious, nesting in colonies in oak groves and streamside woodlands. They are members of the Crow and Jay Family, and like those normally shy birds, are attracted to parks and picnic sites where they can easily be observed feeding on food scraps.

Horned Lark - male

Cliff Swallows - pair at nest

Yellow-billed Magpie

Water Pipit
Anthus spinoletta   6 1/2"

This brown, streaked species is a common winter resident of bare fields and beaches. Habits are similar to the Horned Lark in that pipits walk, and often gather in large flocks, and have similar, white outer-tail feathers. Call notes frequently given are two-syllabled, *pipit*, as if announcing its name. Breeding areas are in the Arctic tundra and high mountain plateaus of North America.

Blue Grosbeak
Guiraca caerulea   6 3/4"

These grosbeaks are summer residents of overgrown fields and thickets, frequently near streams, where they build their nests, low to the ground, in dense shrubs or trees. In poor light, males appear black but their large bills are distinctive. Wintering grounds are in Mexico and Central America. The population of this species has declined in recent years, because of habitat destruction due to suburban growth and parasitism by cowbirds.

Water Pipit - winter

Blue Grosbeak - male

Blue Grosbeak - female and nestlings

Loggerhead Shrike   *Lanius ludovicianus* 9"

Shrikes superficially resemble Mockingbirds, having similar colors and patterns. These birds reside in open country, as well as desert, with scattered trees and brush, and are often seen perched alone, conspicuously, on exposed branches, fence posts or wires. They have a swift, undulating flight and feed on insects, mice and small birds. Loggerhead Shrikes frequently impale their prey on sharp thorns or barbed wire, storing it for later consumption.

European Starling   *Sturnus vulgaris* 8 1/2"

The starling is found naturally throughout Europe and western Asia, and was introduced in New York City a century ago. Since that time, it has spread across North America, and is abundant in a variety of habitats. Although wary of humans, it is bold and aggressive toward other birds, frequently usurping nesting sites of native species, especially those that nest in holes. After the breeding season, this bird gathers in large flocks often in company of blackbirds and cowbirds. In fall and winter, male and female starlings have speckled plumage, and their bills turn dark. Insects, grain and food scraps are almost entirely consumed on the ground. The voice is a chorus of squeaks, chirps and whistles, often imitating calls of other birds and even mocking loud noises.

Lark Sparrow   *Chondestes grammacus* 6 1/2"

These are perhaps the most beautiful of North American sparrows, and one of our finest singers, with a song consisting of a long series of liquid trills and phrases. Nesting is on the ground, well concealed by dense vegetation. Black central tail feathers with prominent white corners and edges, are conspicuous in flight. These large sparrows are resident in southern California throughout the year. In fall and winter, they gather in flocks in weedy fields and along roadsides, feeding on seeds and insects.

Loggerhead Shrike

European Starling - breeding adult

Lark Sparrow

Savannah Sparrow   *Passerculus sandwichensis*   5 1/2"

One of our most abundant sparrows, Savannah Sparrows are birds of grasslands and marshes. There are a number of forms which vary slightly in size, color, and bill size, found in southern California at various seasons and localities, but all have the same basic pattern and habits. These sparrows have a short, erratic flight, and will quickly drop to the ground out of sight and run away through dense vegetation.

Western Meadowlark   *Sturnella neglecta*   9 1/2"

Not a member of the Lark Family, but closely related to blackbirds and orioles, it's a bird of grasslands, cultivated fields and pastures. The wary meadowlark is a ground nester and builds a well-concealed nest, covered by grass or weeds. In fall and winter, family groups travel and feed together. The male sings an exuberant, flute-like, bubbling song, from a conspicuous perch. Meadowlarks' flight resemble that of quails, with quick wing flaps between short sails, displaying prominent white tail corners.

Brown-headed Cowbird   *Molothrus ater*   7 1/2"

Female cowbirds are gray-brown above with paler underparts, and have become the bane of many small birds. Instead of building nests of their own, females lay a single egg in each of ten to twelve nests belonging to other species. Cowbird eggs hatch first, giving their chicks a headstart. Then the young usurpers, taking advantage of larger size, seize proffered food and starve, or push out, rightful nestlings. Host parent birds are unable to recognize this parasitism. Later, adults and fledged young gather in cultivated fields, often associating with livestock. With great increases in agricultural activities, cowbirds have multiplied substantially. This phenomenon, added to widespread destruction of natural habitats, has put tremendous detrimental pressure on songbirds, driving several species to the point of extinction in some areas.

Savannah Sparrow

Western Meadowlark

Brown-headed Cowbird - male

Salton Sea, Imperial County

Birds Included in Chapter V

Long-eared Owl
Black Phoebe
Yellow-breasted Chat
Lazuli Bunting
Song Sparrow
Common Loon
Eared Grebe
Western Grebe
Pied-billed Grebe
American White Pelican
Brown Pelican
Double-crested Cormorant
American Bittern
Great Blue Heron
Great Egret
Snowy Egret
Green-backed Heron
Black-crowned Night-Heron
Wood Stork
Snow Goose
Canada Goose
Brant
Mallard
Green-winged Teal
Blue-winged Teal
Cinnamon Teal
Northern Pintail
Northern Shoveler
American Wigeon
Canvasback
Lesser Scaup
Surf Scoter
Red-breasted Merganser
Ruddy Duck
Osprey

Virginia Rail
Common Moorhen
American Coot
Black-bellied Plover
Snowy Plover
Killdeer
Black Oystercatcher
Black-necked Stilt
American Avocet
Lesser Yellowlegs
Willet
Long-billed Curlew
Marbled Godwit
Black Turnstone
Sanderling
Western Sandpiper
Long-billed Dowitcher
Common Snipe
Wilson's Phalarope
Bonaparte's Gull
Ring-billed Gull
Heermann's Gull
California Gull
Western Gull
Caspian Tern
Forster's Tern
Least Tern
Black Tern
Black Skimmer
Belted Kingfisher
Marsh Wren
Common Yellowthroat
Red-winged Blackbird
Yellow-headed Blackbird
Great-tailed Grackle

108

Chapter V

Birds of the Pacific Coast and Wetlands

The chapter's first section illustrates birds seen in riparian habitats—wooded and shrubby margins along streams, rivers and small bodies of water. This sub-habitat is widely distributed and therefore species favoring these moist areas have non-contiguous ranges.

Larger open bodies of water such as marshes, bays, lakes, ocean coastline, and adjacent land areas, along with Colorado River and Salton Sea environs, make up the second portion. Drainage, channeling, pollution, and development have altered ninety percent of natural wetland and other coastal resources, to the detriment of flora and fauna. Despite this destruction, many water areas, including those created by man, support a surprising quantity and variety of birds.

In fall, winter and spring, the relatively few, specialized residents of wetlands are joined by multitudes of migrant and wintering species. Loons, ducks, geese, shorebirds, herons, gulls, terns, and others are among birds that winter there or at least rest and feed during their migration.

A popular misconception is that all gulls are one species called "Sea Gull." There are many varieties of these birds as shown by several examples in this chapter. In mixed flocks of shorebirds, various sizes indicate presence of fully grown individuals of separate species, rather than small birds being the young of larger ones. Different lengths and shapes of bills enable a variety of species to utilize several food resources in one area at the same time, without directly competing with each another.

Throughout southern California, the best places to see great masses of birds are wetlands. The sight of huge flocks of waterfowl and swarms of shorebirds, wheeling and turning in coordinated flight, is dazzling to eye and mind.

Riparian (streamside) Woodlands

Long-eared Owl — *Asio otus* 15"

Medium size, slender owls with long, close-set "ear" tufts, these birds roost, sometimes several together, close to tree trunks in dense groves during daytime. At night, they hunt over open fields, forest clearings, and marshes for rodents. Nests, often used for several years, are placed in those abandoned by crows, hawks, herons or squirrels. The breeding population has declined recently because of widespread clearing of riparian woodland—their prime habitat.

Black Phoebe — *Sayornis nigricans* 6 3/4"

Always found near water, this common flycatcher is frequently observed standing on a low, exposed perch wagging its tail, then sallying out to catch insects in air or on the ground. A mud cup, mixed with grass, makes up its nest, which is built on a bridge ledge or other man-made structure. The Black Phoebe does not undertake a lengthy migration, but travels short distances after breeding. There is no difference in plumage of male and female adults, but juveniles have some brown as well as black feathers.

Yellow-breasted Chat — *Icteria virens* 7 1/2"

The largest member of the Wood Warbler family is common, but seldom seen, because of its shyness. It inhabits lowland, dense thickets and brush, usually near water. A call, often heard day or night, is composed of repeated clear, varying whistles alternating with harsh notes. This chat migrates through the desert, and spends winter in Mexico and Central America. There are only slight differences in male and female plumage.

Long-eared Owl

Black Phoebe

Yellow-breasted Chat

Lazuli Bunting
Passerina amoena   5 1/2"

   When wintering in Mexico, the male looks like the female, gradually attaining its blue breeding plumage while migrating in spring. This bunting inhabits mixed woodlands and thickets, especially near water. Nests are woven cups of coarse, dried grass, lined with finer grass and hair, built low in thick bushes. Perched at treetop, the male sings his song in fast, high pitched, varied phrases. This species feeds primarily on seeds and insects.

Song Sparrow
Melospiza melodia   6 1/4"

   Appropriately named, this sparrow's attractive song is a mixed, long series of short, sweet and buzzy notes, often given from an exposed perch. The Song Sparrow is a common resident of dense, streamside thickets and marshes. Several races of this species are found in southern California, depending on season and locality, which vary in size, shades of grays and browns, and degree of streaking. All have similar habits and songs.

Lazuli Bunting - male

Lazuli Bunting - female

Song Sparrow

Other Wetlands

Common Loon
Gavia immer 32"

Three species of loons regularly winter in southern California. The large Common Loon is the one most likely to be found on inland waterways. Nesting grounds in North America range from Alaska to Greenland, south to northern United States. Breeding plumage—seldom seen in our area—is a glossy black head and black-and-white checkered back. The expression "crazy as a loon" is based on the strange, undulating, laughter-like yodel, given during the breeding season.

Eared Grebe
Podiceps nigricollis 12 1/2"

Abundant winter visitors and common summer residents, Eared Grebes are seen in a variety of water habitats, from inland to the coast. Nests are built on floating platforms anchored to living vegetation, in shallow open marshes where there is little variation in water levels. While swimming, adults often carry downy chicks on their backs. Grebes feed on insects at water's surface or dive for small fish. Sexes appear alike.

Common Loon - winter

Eared Grebe - breeding

Eared Grebe - winter

Western Grebe *Aechmophorus occidentalis* 25"

This species is found in coastal waters and interior lakes, fall through spring. The similar Clark's Grebe (Chapter VI), is paler, has a yellow-orange bill rather than the Western Grebe's greenish bill, and is more likely to be seen here in summer. Food consists mostly of fish, some insects and, strangely, feathers. The mating display in early spring is a spectacular sight, with pairs actually running together upright, across the water.

Pied-billed Grebe *Podilymbus podiceps* 13 1/2"

Pied-billed Grebes do not gather in large concentrations like Eared Grebes, and frequent freshwater habitats more often than saltwater areas. These birds swim like ducks and usually escape danger by diving, instead of flying. Well concealed floating nests are constructed of reeds attached to aquatic plants in shallow water. In winter, the black on the chin is replaced by white, and the bill changes from black-and-white to dull yellow.

American White Pelican *Pelecanus erythrorhynchos* 62"

These, our biggest birds, winter in great numbers on large, inland bodies of water, especially at the Salton Sea, with a few appearing in coastal areas. Groups of White Pelicans often fish together, dipping their bills in unison. Bill horns and head crests are present only during spring mating season. Nesting areas are on islands in lakes, scattered across the continent, north of southern California. Hundreds of these huge birds often present a marvelous sight, soaring in formation, high in the sky.

Western Grebe

Pied-billed Grebe - breeding　　　　**American White Pelican - breeding**

Brown Pelican *Pelecanus occidentalis* 48"

Brown Pelicans are usually confined to coastal areas and offshore islands, but some can be found at the Salton Sea. Young birds are browner than adults, and have a white belly.these pelicans dive into water, often from great heights, to capture fish. The population declined in recent years because ingested pesticides caused thinned eggshells to crush when adults incubated. With reduced agricultural use of such poisons as DDT entering the ocean in runoff ground water, the number of pelicans is slowly increasing.

Double-crested Cormorant *Phalacrocorax auritus* 32"

Head plumes, which can be white or black, are present only during the breeding season. Double-crested Cormorants are one of three species of cormorants regularly found in California, but it's the only species that lives on inland waters, in addition to coastal habitats. Young birds are brown above, paler on necks and breasts. Cormorant feathers are not completely waterproof, and after diving for fish, these birds frequently perch facing the sun, spreading their wings to dry.

American Bittern *Botaurus lentiginosus* 28"

When assuming a vertical stance with neck outstretched, and long bill pointed upward, the cryptic color and pattern make this fairly common member of the heron family difficult to observe. This is a solitary bird confined to dense marsh vegetation at the Salton Sea, and coastal bays and estuaries, where it feeds on amphibians, reptiles, fish, and insects. A territorial male's booming call is a typical spring marsh sound and carries over great distances.

Brown Pelican - breeding adult

Double-crested Cormorant　　　　　**American Bittern**

Great Blue Heron
Ardea herodias 46"

Our largest heron is often incorrectly called "Blue Crane." Herons fly with their necks folded back, rather than extended as cranes do. The Great Blue Heron hunts both day and night, either by standing motionless in shallow water and waiting for prey to come within striking distance, or actively stalking in wet areas. The nest is a flimsy platform of sticks, built in trees, and often used for several years, in colonies sometimes including other heron species.

Great Egret
Casmerodius albus 39"

The beautiful feathers of the nuptial plumage were in such demand by the millinery trade in the early part of this century, that Great Egrets were almost extirpated from the United States. Strict protection has enabled them to recover to the present status of fairly common. A cosmopolitan species, it is found all over the world in suitable habitats. Nesting and feeding activities are similar to other herons.

Snowy Egret
Egretta thula 24"

The black bill, yellow feet, and smaller size, distinguish this egret from the Great Egret. This species was also decimated by plume hunters. Although now widespread and common, breeding in southern California, especially at the Salton Sea, has declined recently because increasing numbers of more aggressive Cattle Egrets are usurping limited, prime nesting sites in dense marshes. Egrets are members of the Heron and Bittern Family.

Great Blue Heron

Great Egret

Snowy Egret

Green-backed Heron   *Butorides striatus*   18"

This small heron is more solitary than other members of its family. A widespread resident, it usually prefers healthy riparian growth, rather than open marshes. The nest is a platform of sticks, lined with finer twigs, in willow thickets or other dense brush. When fishing, a Green-backed Heron sits motionless at the water's edge, poised to strike. Sometimes it uses feathers and insects as "fishing lures."

Black-crowned Night-Heron   *Nycticorax nycticorax*   25"

Although largely nocturnal, groups composed of young birds and adults are often seen roosting together in daytime. Night-Herons are extremely adaptable, nesting with other herons as well as alone, in marshes and stands of tall trees. Nests are flimsy platforms of sticks, scantily lined with finer materials. Food is varied and, along with the usual heron diet of fish, includes rodents, succulent plants, and even small birds.

Green-backed Heron

Black-crowned Night-Heron - adult

Black-crowned Night-Heron - juvenile

Wood Stork *Mycteria americana* 40"

Several species of water birds nest in Mexico and fly north after the breeding season. These dispersers are usually young birds; among them are Wood Storks. Storks begin arriving in numbers at the Salton Sea's southern end in late May. On rare occasions, they visit the seacoast, north to Santa Barbara County and beyond. Generally by September, they have returned to Mexico.

Snow Goose *Chen caerulescens* 28"

An arctic tundra nester, large numbers winter near the Salton Sea with individuals seen in scattered locations elsewhere. The immature bird's head and back are grayish and it has a dark bill. A blue phase is called Blue Goose. This type was considered a distinct species until evidence showed it's merely a genetic variant. The Snow Goose diet, while on wintering grounds, consists of waste grain and aquatic plants.

Canada Goose *Branta canadensis* 45"

The natural breeding range of Canada Geese extends from arctic slopes south to northern California, but semi-wild, or injured individuals sometimes nest in local protected areas. This species frequents wetland habitats near fields accessible for foraging. Several subspecies ranging in size from twenty-five inches to forty-five inches, occasionally winter in southern California. Color, pattern, and habits are basically the same in all types. Geese maintain strong family ties—young remaining with adults until the next breeding season.

Wood Storks

Snow Goose

Canada Goose

Brant *Branta bernicla* 25"

Brant are true sea geese and have salt glands enabling them to drink ocean water. They are generally confined to the Pacific coast, but a few regularly appear on large inland waters, such as the Salton Sea, especially in spring and summer. Preferred food is eelgrass which only grows in shallow estuaries, but they also eat other aquatic vegetation, crustaceans and insects. Flocks winter locally on bays, river mouths and estuaries, migrating north to nesting areas on the coasts of arctic Alaska, from March to May.

Mallard *Anas platyrhynchos* 23"

Purposeful releases and escaped birds from parks and private aviaries make it difficult to determine which individuals are wild. Our most familiar duck has become well-known as the result of widespread, captive breeding. This practice has produced many strange combinations of colors and shapes. The Mallard is found throughout the world's temperate regions, and in North America, the greatest nesting concentrations are in Canada's prairie provinces.

Brant

Mallard - male

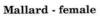

Mallard - female

Green-winged Teal
Anas crecca   14 1/2"

Our smallest, surface-feeding duck is common in fall, winter and spring, in shallow freshwater and brackish habitats. It is wary, and will not tolerate close approach. The female is mostly brown, but has bright green patches on the trailing edges of her wings. Breeding grounds are in Alaska, Canada, and northern United States. Diet includes aquatic vegetation and seeds. Sometimes it walks long distances on land in search of food.

Blue-winged Teal
Anas discors   15 1/2"

The male is identified by a distinctive white crescent on his face, and sky blue wing patches. The female is almost identical to the female Cinnamon Teal, both having blue on their wings. Once considered rare in southern California, this bird has become more common in recent years, particularly in the spring and fall, on marshy ponds and coastal estuaries. Normal breeding range is from southern, interior United States north to Canada.

Cinnamon Teal
Anas cyanoptera   16"

This teal is a common migrant, and summer resident in southern California, on virtually any freshwater marsh and coastal estuary, with a few remaining throughout winter. The favored location for the nest—a depression lined with grass and concealed by woven vegetation—is a marsh or adjacent meadow. The male is distinctive, but the female resembles other small female ducks. Food is primarily aquatic vegetation, insects and crustaceans.

Green-winged Teal - male

Blue-winged Teal - male

Cinnamon Teal - male

Northern Pintail
Anas acuta 26"

A plentiful duck, the pintail is found in both freshwater and saltwater environments. It occasionally nests locally, but the majority migrate to Alaska, Canada, and northern United States to breed. This bird feeds with its tail straight up, and uses its long neck to reach for aquatic plants, below the water's surface—a common trait of dabbling ducks. The female has a slender, more delicate appearance than other female ducks.

Northern Shoveler
Anas clypeata 19"

The spoon-shaped bill readily identifies both sexes of this duck. It feeds in shallow waters, using comblike "teeth" on the edges of its bill to strain tiny plants and animals. Like many ducks, this species undergoes a plumage change immediately after the breeding season, when the male attains a female-like appearance, called "eclipse" plumage. Often, all the colorful flight feathers are molted and the bird is unable to fly for a few weeks until new ones are grown. The female goes through a change too, but her appearance remains much the same. Full breeding regalia is regained in late fall and winter.

American Wigeon
Anas americana 19"

Being grazers, wigeons forage in open, grassy areas for young grass and grain, as well as feeding on aquatic plants in shallow water. They are common in winter, but rare in summer. These birds range with other ducks into mountains, unless severe weather drives them to lower elevations. Females are brown, and separated from other species by their short, pale gray bills. Nesting grounds are in Alaska, western Canada and northern United States.

Northern Pintail - male

Northern Shoveler - male

American Wigeon - male

Canvasback   *Aythya valisineria*   21"

The name refers to the male's pale gray back and white sides, dotted with a wave-like pattern, resembling canvas fabric. Sloping foreheads and long dark bills are characteristic of both sexes, but the female has a pale brown head and neck with a brownish-gray back and sides. Aquatic vegetation is the staple food, but it's also fond of straining seeds from bottom mud with its bill, consequently, lead is ingested from spent shotgun shells. This poisoning, combined with the draining of northern marshes where it breeds, has caused a dramatic population decline.

Lesser Scaup   *Aythya affinis*   16 1/2"

In good light, the males' head often show a purple gloss. Females are brown overall, with white patches surrounding the bills. These are common, diving ducks, feeding equally on plants and tiny aquatic creatures. Breeding areas are in marshes of the prairie country, from eastern Alaska through western Canada, and northern United States. They winter on both coastal and interior bodies of water.

Surf Scoter   *Melanitta perspicillata*   20"

An abundant winter visitant and spring transient, this scoter is normally confined to coastal waters, but occasionally is seen on interior lakes and the Salton Sea. It typically plunges into breaking waves along the shore, diving to depths of thirty feet, for its favorite food—mollusks. The female is brown with white patches near the bill and behind the eye on each side of her face. Principal nesting areas are on tundra in Alaska and northern Canada.

Canvasback - male

Lesser Scaup - male

Surf Scoter - male

Red-breasted Merganser *Mergus serrator* 23"

Mergansers have long, narrow bills with backward projecting teeth, which enable them to grasp and hold fish, their primary food. Red-breasted Mergansers are winter residents in coastal waters, and breed in the far northern regions of the continent. They are among the swiftest of ducks in flight, as well as when swimming. Females and young are mostly brown, and have smaller white wing patches than males.

Ruddy Duck *Oxyura jamaicensis* 15"

This beautiful duck is common year-round in most areas. The male's breeding plumage is retained briefly, from about April to August, when he resumes his basic plumage which resembles the female's, but lacking the dark line she has through her cheek patch. The male's long tail is often cocked in any season. Most food— aquatic vegetation, insects and snails—is obtained by straining from soft mud. The Ruddy Duck's range is widespread, and is one of few species of waterfowl to breed in both North and South America.

Red-breasted Merganser - male

Ruddy Duck - breeding male

Ruddy Duck - winter female

Osprey   *Pandion haliaetus*   23 1/2", wingspread 65"

The Osprey is distributed worldwide. In southern California, it is found in coastal areas and around larger, interior bodies of water. Strictly a fish eater, it has toes with strong talons and a special coarse surface, enabling it to catch and grasp its slippery prey. This bird of prey flies with its wings in a characteristic crook, and often hovers just before plunging for a fish. Conservation programs and reduced use of agricultural pesticides have stopped the decline of this species.

Virginia Rail   *Rallus limicola*   9 1/2"

Rails are compact chicken-like birds of marshes. Solitary and secretive, they are more often heard than seen. Calls most frequently given, are a series of loud, metallic notes combined with various grunting sounds. Their narrow bodies enable them to move easily through dense, marsh vegetation. Nests are loosely woven cups of coarse grasses, fastened to clumps of plants or on tussocks, just above mud or water. Virginia Rails probe mud with their long bills for earthworms, insects, and snails.

Common Moorhen   *Gallinula chloropus*   14"

This species was, until recently, called Common Gallinule, but the name was changed to conform with that used in other parts of the world. It's not as shy as most other rails, but can often be seen swimming in open water, or walking on exposed land and floating plants. While swimming, the head is pumped back and forth. The nest is a mass of dead stems, sometimes floating, anchored to a bush. Downy young are black, with black-tipped red bills.

Osprey

Virginia Rail

Common Moorhen

American Coot　　　　　*Fulica americana*　15 1/2"

This abundant bird, nicknamed "Mud Hen," is found in all kinds of wetlands, even grazing on greens of golf courses and grassy areas surrounding ponds and lakes. Its toes are lobed—about half as webbed as a duck. Young birds range from black, when a chick, to pale gray as a juvenile.They're expert swimmers and divers, feeding on a variety of plant and animal food. The call, consisting of loud cackles, croaks and whistles, is uttered day and night. Recordings of these vocalizations are often used as background in sound tracks of jungle or swamp movies and television shows.

Black-bellied Plover　　　*Pluvialis squatarola*　11 1/2"

For Californians, this bird is not well-named, because when seen here in winter, this plover's underparts are grayish. Breeding plumage is attained in late spring, and then its black face, breast, and belly is striking. Nesting grounds are on arctic tundra. Black axillaries (armpits), seen in flight, distinguish this species in all plumages. The Black-bellied Plover is one of our most numerous shorebirds, and frequents rocky shores, sandy beaches, and mud flats.

Snowy Plover　　　*Charadrius alexandrinus*　6 1/4"

These are fairly common little birds of coastal, sandy beaches, along with gravel and dry alkaline shorelines of interior waters, such as the Salton Sea. Quite tame, they allow close approach, preferring to run away, rather than fly. Nests are mere hollows in the ground, lined with small shells. The population at the coast has declined considerably because of disturbance of their restricted habitat. Females and young are more uniform brown with little or none of the male's black head markings.

American Coot

Black-bellied Plovers - winter

Snowy Plover - breeding male

Killdeer   *Charadrius vociferus*   10 1/2"

Double breast bands on both male and female are distinguishing marks of this widespread and common plover. Cultivated fields, mud flats, grassy open areas, and even gravel roofs are among many places this species breeds. Its nest is a slight depression, lined with pebbles and grasses. Like many shorebirds, it will feign a broken wing to lure intruders away from its nest or young. It is extremely vocal, and on close approach, it repeatedly emits a piercing call that sounds like its name, frightening off most other birds that are in the vicinity, much to the dismay of birders and photographers.

Black Oystercatcher   *Haematopus bachmani*   17 1/2"

This species is fairly common on the rocky coast of Santa Barbara County and the Channel Islands, but rarer further south. It uses its highly specialized bill to pry open mussels, marine worms, and other shellfish. The oystercatcher does not migrate, but in winter, sometimes gathers in small flocks, staying fairly close to nesting sites. The sexes look alike, but adults have dark plumage and totally bright red-orange bills rather than partial dusky of immatures.

Black-necked Stilt   *Himantopus mexicanus*   14"

A conspicuous and abundant species, this bird nests on dryer sections near foraging areas of shallow lakeshores, flooded fields, mud flats, and coastal estuaries. Nesting is on the ground in loose colonies. It is extremely vocal, emitting a loud *kek   kek   kek*, especially in the vicinity of its nest. As with most shorebirds, the young are precocial, able to feed and take care of themselves soon after hatching. Female plumage is like the male's, but she has a brownish back instead of the male's jet black, and is overall duller.

Killdeer

Black Oystercatcher - immature

Black-necked Stilt - male

American Avocet   *Recurvirostra americana*   18"

Sweeping its upturned bill rapidly from side to side, often in unison with other avocets, it feeds on stirred-up aquatic insects. Foraging areas are similar to the Black-necked Stilt, but this bird will wade, and even swim, into deeper water. Although a common, year-round visitor to southern California, it nests further north in the state. The cinnamon color is present only during courting and nesting, then afterwards fades to dusky white. Females' bills are more sharply upturned than males'.

Lesser Yellowlegs   *Tringa flavipes*   10 1/2"

There are two similar sandpipers named "yellowlegs," after their conspicuous, bright yellow legs—Lesser Yellowlegs and the other species which is larger, Greater Yellowlegs. Both are common transients, but Lessers are rare in winter. This species is partial to coastal estuaries, flooded fields and mud flats. The fine streaks of its breeding plumage become smudged and faded in fall. Nesting is in open muskeg sections of spruce forests, from Alaska to northern Canada.

Willet   *Catoptrophorus semipalmatus*   15"

The drab appearance of both male and female Willets when standing, gives no hint of the striking black-and-white pattern displayed in flight.These birds frequent coastal and Salton Sea shorelines in winter, but a few non-breeders remain through summer. Conspicuous, noisy birds, they repeatedly give calls that sound like *pill-will-willet*. Nesting areas are mainly in the prairie country of Canada and northern United States.

American Avocet - male

Lesser Yellowlegs - breeding *

Willet - winter

Long-billed Curlew *Numenius americanus* 23"

This is another example of specialized bills in the Sandpiper Family. Largest of that group is the Long-billed Curlew which uses its distinctive bill to probe deeply into mud for small mollusks and other invertebrates, swallowing them whole. Preferred winter habitats are coastal estuaries and inland agricultural fields. This species is often gregarious, and migrating flocks can be observed moving north in spring to nest, calling loudly, a chorus of plaintive notes sounding like *cur-lee*.

Marbled Godwit *Limosa fedoa* 18"

Godwits have long upturned bills, as opposed to downturned bills of curlews. There are sensitive nerves in the bill tips, enabling these birds to feed by feel as they probe mud for worms and crustaceans. Characteristic wintering birds of open shore, mud flats and marshes, usually near the coast, they're also common at the Salton Sea. They nest in grassy meadows of northwestern North America.

Black Turnstone *Arenaria melanocephala* 9 1/4"

During winter, this is a characteristic bird of rocky coasts, debris-littered beaches and breakwaters. The name comes from the habit of turning over stones, shells, clods of dirt, and seaweed in search of small, marine animals. Juvenile and winter adults are slate gray, without the face spot and eye stripe. In flight, it displays a conspicuous black-and-white pied pattern in all seasons. The coast and offshore islands of Alaska are nesting sites.

Long-billed Curlew

Marbled Godwit

Black Turnstone

Sanderling
Calidris alba 8"

These are little birds that chase back and forth, following edges of waves on beaches. In winter, when observed here, they are the palest of sandpipers. Sanderlings also frequent rocky shores and coastal estuaries, rarely away from the coast and then, most often, at the Salton Sea. Prolific travelers, their range extends from northern breeding areas on the arctic slope of Canada, to wintering grounds in southern South America.

Western Sandpiper
Calidris mauri 6 1/2"

Collectively, the various species of small sandpipers are called "peeps." Western Sandpipers are perhaps the most abundant of the group. Identification of individual sandpipers is one of the great challenges of birding, but with study and practice, these small birds can be properly named. The difficulty lies with subtle plumage variations taking place gradually from breeding adults into winter plumage, back to breeding. Additional confusion arises from juveniles of many species changing into adults as they migrate through southern California, and also, appearances vary because of normal wear, tear and loss of feathers.

Long-billed Dowitcher
Limnodromus scolopaceus 11 1/2"

The white lower back and rump identify this species and its close relative, the Short-billed Dowitcher. The two species are similar in appearance and feeding habits—both probe mud with long bills for insects, mollusks and plant food. They are best told apart by their calls. The Short-billed Dowitcher makes a quick series of three soft notes, sounding like *tu-tu-tu*, while the Long-billed has a single sharp *keek*, given singly or in fairly rapid succession. Both species are transients and winter visitors, with nesting taking place in far northern portions of the continent.

146

Sanderlings - winter

Western Sandpiper - juvenile

Long-billed Dowitchers

Common Snipe
Gallinago gallinago   10 1/2"

This is a common, but inconspicuous bird of wet meadows and marshy edges of streams and ponds. Often a snipe will remain hidden until closely approached, then explode into a fast, zigzag flight, and drop out of sight at some distance into the marsh. The pliable, serrated bill, along with spikes on the tongue, enable this bird to feed on insects, mollusks, and crustaceans. The snipe is a winter bird in southern California, and nests from northern California, north to Canada and Alaska.

Wilson's Phalarope
Phalaropus tricolor   9 1/4"

Phalaropes are sandpipers with several unique characteristics. Breeding plumage of females are brighter than males, but in fall, both look like the juvenile illustrated. After mating, males build nests, incubate eggs and care for young. Phalaropes are equally comfortable wading or swimming. When swimming, they often spin like tops, rapidly dabbing disturbed water with their long, thin bills, eating aquatic insects. Wilson's Phalaropes nest in the western prairie country of the United States and Canada. Winter is spent primarily in western South America, with few remaining in our area. Mono Lake, California, is an important migration stop, where, seasonally, thousands of these birds rest and devour abundant brine flies.

Common Snipe

Wilson's Phalarope - breeding female

Wilson's Phalarope - juvenile

Bonaparte's Gull
Larus philadelphia 13 1/2"

Often gathering in large flocks, these small gulls are common winter visitors, primarily along the coast with some migration through the interior. Their flight is lighter and more buoyant than other gulls. In late spring, the winter adult's white head changes to black. Young birds have black- tipped tails, and appear more dusky. Most gulls are ground-nesters, but this species is unusual in that its nest is built in a tree. They are summer residents of northern spruce-fir forests.

Ring-billed Gull
Larus delawarensis 17 1/2"

Its name comes from a black ring around the middle of the adult's bill. Like most gulls, young birds are brown becoming lighter as they mature. The least oceanic of our gulls, they are commonly observed all year in inland urban areas, as well as coastal regions. Numbers have increased due to availability of garbage in places such as dumps. Individuals seen in summer are non-breeders, as the nesting grounds are in northwestern United States and central Canada.

Bonaparte's Gull - breeding

Bonaparte's Gull - winter adult

Ring-billed Gull - adult

Heermann's Gull
Larus heermanni 19"

The striking combination of dark gray body, white head and red bill of adults make this the easiest of western gulls to identify. Immature birds are the darkest of gulls. Nesting is on rocky islands off the Mexican coast, with post-breeding individuals arriving in southern California in late May, and returning to Mexico about mid-February. Heermann's Gulls are common along the coast and only casual inland.

California Gull
Larus californicus 21"

This species is often seen flying in flocks over urban centers in winter. It is an abundant bird from western inland valleys and along the coast, to well out at sea. Elsewhere in southern California, it is primarily a transient, with non-breeding individuals remaining through summer. This is the gull that helped save early Mormans in Utah, by eating crickets, during their plague of 1848. A major nesting area is located at Mono Lake, one of many reasons why this unique, natural region should be preserved.

Heermann's Gull - breeding

Heermann's Gull - first winter

California Gull - adult

Western Gull
Larus occidentalis 25"

These are large gulls, observed commonly along the immediate seacoast, year-round. They are colonial ground nesters on the Channel Islands and are the only gull species that breeds in our area. Young take four years to reach maturity and follow the usual gull pattern of dark brown immatures gradually attaining the adult whiter plumage. These birds are fond of following boats, scavenging food scraps and bait thrown overboard.

Caspian Tern
Sterna caspia 21"

Terns are closely related to gulls, but are streamlined and more graceful in flight. This species is the largest of California terns, and feeds by diving from the air, for small fish. The Caspian Tern is found worldwide, but in our area, nests only in San Diego County. Breeding adults have black caps, but crowns are dusky on immatures and winter adults. A common transient, and winter and summer visitor, it frequents coastal areas and freshwater lakes.

Western Gull - adult

Western Gull - juvenile

Caspian Tern - breeding adult with chick

Forster's Tern *Sterna forsteri* 14 1/2"

This graceful tern loses its black cap after the nesting season, but retains a black patch on each side of its head. The Forster's Tern can be seen in most wetland areas of southern California, in all seasons. A major nesting colony is in San Diego County, but it has also nested at the Salton Sea. This species catches insects in air and off water, in addition to diving for fish. Like most gulls and terns, sexes are alike.

Least Tern *Sterna antillarum* 9"

Numbers of this smallest of American terns have declined in recent years, because of human disturbance of breeding sites. Flat, open areas along the coast, with nearby fishing waters, are required for nesting. As seen in the photograph, the nest is quite simple, usually a mere scrape in the ground, lined with a stick or two. Winter is spent in coastal regions from Mexico south to northern South America.

Black Tern *Chlidonias niger* 9 3/4"

Our only completely black-colored tern molts into its winter plumage—white head and underparts—by midsummer. This species breeds in marshy areas of the San Joaquin Valley, just north of our region, and across the United States and Canada. Flight is erratic and buoyant with frequent hovering. Food includes insects caught on wing as well as the usual tern prey of small fish snatched from water. Huge flocks of these terns can be seen, fall and spring, in transit at the Salton Sea, and in smaller numbers at inland lakes and marshes during other seasons.

Forster's Tern - breeding

Least Tern - breeding

Black Terns - breeding

Black Skimmer *Rynchops niger* 18"

A recent arrival to southern California, this species is seen, with increasing frequency, along the coast and at the Salton Sea, with new nesting areas being established regularly. Reasons for this phenomenal increase are a mystery, because nearest previous known breeding colonies are several hundred miles south in Mexico. This is the only bird with the lower part of its bill markedly longer than the upper. It feeds by skimming low over water, with the bill open and partially submerged, then, on striking a small crustacean or fish, the upper mandible clamps down on the prey.

Belted Kingfisher *Ceryle alcyon* 13"

Large, ragged crests give this bird a big-headed appearance. Females have rufous flanks, and chestnut bands across their bellies, in addition to the single, blue-gray breast band of males. Kingfishers catch fish by diving into water, either from perches or by hovering and then diving. These wary birds do not allow close approach, and hide their nests at the inside end of deep, horizontal burrows that they dig in earthern banks of streams, lakes or other water courses. Their call is a loud, harsh rattle, frequently given in flight. Belted Kingfishers are widespread visitants, but rare breeders, in southern California.

Marsh Wren *Cistothorus palustris* 5"

Every cattail marsh seems to have a resident colony of Marsh Wrens. In winter, they frequent wet, brushy areas as well. Nests are built by females, anchored to reeds, and are round, with side entrances. Males often make several roosting nests in the same style and area. Songs are series of loud trills and coarse gurgles, sung day or night, either from perches or when fluttering in air. Sexes look alike.

Black Skimmer

Belted Kingfisher - male

Marsh Wren

Common Yellowthroat   *Geothlypis trichas*   5"

The female lacks the male's black mask. A breeding resident of marshes and wet, weedy growth, difficult to see because it usually stays hidden, the Common Yellowthroat suffers from being a frequent cowbird host (Chapter IV—Brown-headed Cowbird). The song consists of notes sounding like *twitchity, twitchity*. In migration, this warbler can appear in almost any brushy habitat, even in the desert.

Red-winged Blackbird   *Agelaius phoeniceus*   8 3/4"

These birds are typical residents and widespread breeders in cattail marshes, grassy fields and brush. Males establish territories by clinging to tall stalks, displaying their red shoulder patches, and singing a liquid, gurgling succession of phrases. After nesting, Red-winged Blackbirds form flocks, mixing with other blackbird species, and move into agricultural areas. Occasionally, they will come to suburban bird feeders.

Common Yellowthroat - male

Red-winged Blackbird - male

Red-winged Blackbird - female

Yellow-headed Blackbird

Xanthocephalus xanthocephalus   9 1/2"

Although some colonies are scattered along the coast, most are confined to inland marshes. Breeding sites are more specialized than those of Red-winged Blackbirds, and located only where plant habitat is above standing water. After nesting, like other blackbirds, the Yellow-headed Blackbird is more widespread, congregating and moving into agricultural areas. The male's yellow head, in combination with white wing patches, are conspicuous field marks. This bird is aggressive, driving other species from choice areas, and striking hawks, even humans, in the vicinity of its nest.

Great-tailed Grackle   *Quiscalus mexicanus*   18"

A resident of the Colorado River region, this grackle has spread in recent years to the Pacific coast, and north to Death Valley. It is regularly found at the Salton Sea, and has been seen in a number of desert oases and agricultural areas, usually near water. The female and young are much smaller and browner than the male, and lack his keel-shaped tail. Among food included in its varied diet are insects, lizards, bird eggs, fruit and grain, augmented with scraps scavenged in parks and campgrounds. This bird often walks with tail held high, constantly calling a variety of harsh whistles and clucks.

Yellow-headed Blackbird - male

Yellow-headed Blackbird - female

Great-tailed Grackle - male

Birds Included in Chapter VI

Clark's Grebe

Pink-footed Shearwater

Blue-footed Booby

Yellow-crowned Night-Heron

White-faced Ibis

Wood Duck

Eurasian Wigeon

California Condor

Bar-tailed Godwit

Yellow-footed Gull

Elegant Tern

Pigeon Guillemot

Elf Owl

Xantus' Hummingbird

California Gnatcatcher

Bell's Vireo

Yellow-throated Warbler

Blackpoll Warbler

Ovenbird

Tricolored Blackbird

Evening Grosbeak

Chapter VI

Specialized, Rare and Unusual Birds

Southern California's unique location and varied topography make it a prime environment for large numbers of more or less common birds. But several species, once observed frequently, are now scarce or absent altogether, because their breeding and feeding grounds were destroyed by urbanization. Specialized wildlife cannot adapt to new conditions, or simply move elsewhere. If precise habitat requisites are not preserved, certain birds will be eliminated.

In addition, this region acts as a magnet for many rare and unusual species. Some of these are seen on a regular, but limited basis, while others may be a once-in-a-lifetime sighting. These irregular phenomena add to the fascination of birding in our area. However, care should be taken when identifying rare species. Even experienced birders can be confused in their zeal to report an unusual observance.

A few specialties already have been discussed in other chapters. They include Yellow-billed Magpie, Wrentit and Lawrence's Goldfinch. Pictured here are twenty-one more examples of specialized, rare and unusual birds. All photographs were taken in California.

Clark's Grebe   *Aechmophorus clarkii*   25"

This bird was once considered a color phase of the Western Grebe. Recent research has indicated that, where ranges overlap, there is little interbreeding. General habits and appearance are similar, but Clark's Grebe is paler, tends to feed further from shore, and has a single call note, versus the Western Grebes's double note. For additional information, refer to the Western Grebe listing, Chapter V—Wetlands.

Pink-footed Shearwater   *Puffinus creatopus*   19"

Pelagic (or oceanic), is an avian group unfamiliar to many people. Some—for example, storm-petrels—are among the most numerous of the world's birds. Most come to land only during breeding season. Biological adaptations enable them to drink sea water, and travel long distances, with little consumption of energy. Pelagic birds do not wander the open seas aimlessly, but follow a precise pattern, as do land birds. The Pink-footed Shearwater is typical, and nests on islands off the coast of Chile, ranging offshore north to Alaska, from spring into fall. It feeds on small fish, squid and crustaceans.

Blue-footed Booby   *Sula nebouxii*   32"

The post-breeding movement of some Mexican birds is mentioned in the Wood Stork listing, (Chapter V). That phenomenon in the Blue-footed Booby is extremely rare but does happen occasionally. The closest booby breeding grounds are on arid islands in the Gulf of California. Sometimes a Blue- footed Booby is seen at sea, off our coast, but the majority of sightings has been at the Salton Sea, and other inland bodies of water, in late summer.

Clark's Grebe

Pink-footed Shearwater

Blue-footed Booby

Yellow-crowned Night-Heron *Nycticorax violaceus* 24"

These birds are casual stragglers, from early spring to late fall, to coastal marshes. Individuals observed here probably originated in western Mexico, although the species is a regular nesting resident in southeastern United States. Most were adults as pictured, but immatures closely resemble those of Black-crowned Night-Herons (Chapter V) and could possibly be overlooked.

White-faced Ibis *Plegadis chihi* 23"

White-faced Ibises require extensive marshes for nesting, and flooded fields for primary feeding areas. White borders around their bare, red, facial skin are present only in breeding season. In certain locales, these ibises are fairly common, but with continuous destruction of fresh water marshes, the population has declined. Recently a small colony has been established in northern Los Angeles County, and it's hoped, with protection, this group will expand.

Wood Duck *Aix sponsa* 18 1/2"

Considered by many to be our most beautiful duck, this species is often raised in captivity. It is uncommon, but escapes from private collections make the exact wild population status uncertain. Nesting is different from most ducks, with hollows in trees, far from water, generally utilized. Occasionally, these cavities are as high as fifty feet above ground, and man-made nest boxes sometimes are accepted. The female is drab—a mixture of browns and grays, with a white eye ring and gray crest.

Yellow-crowned Night-Heron

White-faced Ibis - breeding

Wood Duck - male

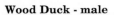

Eurasian Wigeon   *Anas penelope*   20"

Occasionally a Eurasian Wigeon will appear among flocks of American Wigeon (Chapter V) in freshwater lakes or brackish estuaries. Both ducks feed on aquatic plants and graze in grassy areas for seeds. Males of the two species are quite different, but females are almost inseparable. This bird's normal wintering grounds are in Europe, Asia and northeast Africa.

California Condor

Gymnogyps californianus   47", wingspread 108"

Presently, the few remaining condors are in a captive breeding program. The plan is to eventually release birds in protected areas, and with supplemental food supplies, maintain the species. But it's sad that truly wild condors will never again exist. This magnificent vulture has the largest wingspread of any North American land bird, and is a living fossil of the Pleistocene Age, more than a million years ago. In historic times, its range extended from British Columbia, across the United States to Florida. Habitat destruction by changing land use, combined with shooting, and feeding on poisoned predators accounts for the rapid disappearance of modern California Condors.

Bar-tailed Godwit   *Limosa lapponica*   16"

The Bar-tailed Godwit breeds in Alaska, appears casually in migration along the Pacific coast, and normally winters from southern Asia south to Australia and New Zealand. It has been observed in southern California, on a mud flat or sandy beach, associating with other shorebirds. This species resembles the common Marbled Godwit (Chapter V), but is grayer, and smaller, with shorter legs and bill.

170

Eurasian Wigeon - male

California Condor

Bar-tailed Godwit

Yellow-footed Gull
Larus livens   27"

This bird was considered to be a geographic variant of the Western Gull (Chapter V), however, recent research shows it to be a distinct species. A Mexican resident, breeding in the Gulf of California, it regularly appears at the Salton Sea, mostly in summer, but a few also winter. Found nowhere else in the United States, the Yellow-footed Gull is one of our most sought after specialty birds.

Elegant Tern
Sterna elegans   17"

Another species originating in Mexico, this tern now is firmly established in this country, but only in California. San Diego County has a small nesting colony, and an additional one was recently located in Orange County. Most individuals observed during July through October, are post-breeding visitants from Baja California. Feeding areas are bays, estuaries and in-shore coastal waters, but never very far inland.

Pigeon Guillemot
Cepphus columba   13 1/2"

The Auk and Puffin Family—northern counterpart of Southern Hemisphere penguins—are collectively called "alcids." These birds swim and dive expertly for fish, crustaceans and algae. Various species nest on seacliffs, in caves or burrows, and even in forested areas. Pigeon Guillemots, typical examples of this family, are fairly common, summer nesting residents of the northern Channel Islands and on the coast of northern Santa Barbara County. Breeding adults' dark gray plumage changes to white with black-mottled upperparts in fall. Wintering grounds are unknown, but it's suspected they're far at sea.

Yellow-footed Gull - adult

Elegant Tern - breeding

Pigeon Guillemot - breeding

Elf Owl *Micrathene whitneyi* 5 3/4"

This tiny owl barely ranges into our area from Arizona in woodlands along desert water courses, or at desert oases. It uses an abandoned woodpecker hole in a tree or snag for a nesting site, and feeds on insects, small snakes and lizards. Destruction of its scarce habitat, and human disturbance, have virtually eliminated the Elf Owl from California. Attempts have been made to reintroduce this bird in promising locations, with limited success.

Xantus' Hummingbird *Hylocharis xantusii* 3 1/2"

A female of this species appeared at a feeding station in Ventura County in January, 1988, and attracted hundreds of birders from all over the country. This bird made several attempts to nest, but was unsuccessful because of infertile eggs. Normally, the Xantus' Hummingbird is confined to Baja California's southern half, and was never previously known to travel out of its restricted range. Here is one of those unexplained records that makes birding exciting in our region.

California Gnatcatcher *Polioptila californica* 4 1/2"

Until recently this bird was considered a variation of the Black-tailed Gnatcatcher. Research has determined that the two forms are actually separate species because of differences in voices and habits. The California Gnatcatcher, pictured here, is darker and browner than the other species which is a widespread resident of inland desert washes, whereas this bird is restricted to sagebrush on dry coastal slopes from southern California, south into Baja California. Both have black on their tail undersides, instead of white in the similar Blue-gray Gnatcatcher (Chapter III). During winter, when the male's black cap is absent, sexes look alike.

Elf Owl

Xantus' Hummingbird - female

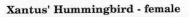

California Gnatcatcher - male

Bell's Vireo   *Vireo bellii*   4 3/4"

The West Coast form, native to southern California, is now rarely found. Its numbers have been greatly reduced by destruction of its preferred habitat—dense willow thickets along streams—combined with parasitism by cowbirds. A summer nester here, it winters in Mexico, migrating through the desert. Other races of this species are resident in central and southern United States and are not as seriously threatened.

Yellow-throated Warbler   *Dendroica dominica*   5 1/2"

Occasionally, especially during migration, a bird will stray a great distance from its normal range, and appear in our region. There is no accepted explanation for this phenomenon. Forested coastal sections and desert oases seem to attract these vagrants. The Yellow-throated Warbler normally is a summer resident in mixed woodlands of southeastern United States. It has been recorded here infrequently, mostly in spring.

Blackpoll Warbler   *Dendroica striata*   5 1/2"

This species is a rare, but regular visitant to our area, especially in fall, when it looks different from the breeding plumaged bird pictured here. Then, it is mostly greenish-yellow, rather than black-and-white. The Blackpoll Warbler nests in coniferous forests of northeastern United States, Canada and Alaska, and usually migrates east of the plains states, to wintering grounds in South America.

Bell's Vireo

Yellow-throated Warbler

Blackpoll Warbler

Ovenbird *Seiurus aurocapillus* 6"

A rare spring and fall visitant to southern California, the Ovenbird has an unusual habit of walking with its tail cocked, searching on the ground for insects, instead of feeding in trees like other warblers. Plumage does not seasonally change and sexes appear alike. Normal breeding range is eastern United States and Canada, with wintering grounds in Central America.

Tricolored Blackbird *Agelaius tricolor* 8 3/4"

This is another California specialty, with its range principally confined to the Golden State. This male differs from the Red-winged Blackbird (Chapter V) by having a white slash below his red shoulder patch. Females of the two are similar, with the Tricolored Blackbird being darker. Large colonies nest in marshes of western portions of southern California. After breeding, it gathers in flocks, sometimes with other blackbirds, and moves into agricultural areas.

Evening Grosbeak *Coccothraustes vespertinus* 8"

The name is based on an incorrect notion they're strictly evening singers, when in fact, their soft warble can be heard at any time of day. Nesting is in coniferous forests, north of our area. Highly gregarious, Evening Grosbeaks are irregular transients and sporadic winter visitors to southern California. Food consists of seeds, fruit and insects, with a special fondness for sunflower seeds. Females are duller than males, tending toward grays and tans, rather than blacks and yellows.

Ovenbird

Tricolored Blackbird - male

Evening Grosbeak - male

Suggested References

An enormous amount of literature is available concerning birds, covering every conceivable facet of ornithology, with more being published constantly. Following are a few publications the author has found useful in the field or in writing this book. These works provide additional details about various aspects of bird study.

American Ornithologists' Union, 1983, Washington, DC, *Check-List of North American Birds*. The standard reference for names, classification and ranges of all species recorded from North America, Central America and Hawaii.

Clarke, Herbert, and Arnold Small, 1976, *Birds of the West*, A.S.Barnes and Co., Cranbury, NJ. Out of print, but copies may be available. A good habitat overview of western United States.

Ehrlich, Paul; David S. Dobkin, and Darryl Wheye, 1988, *The Birder's Handbook*, Simon & Schuster, Inc., New York, NY. Slightly larger than, and a good supplement to field guides. Included are interesting accounts of the natural history of most North American birds, concisely arranged.

Garrett, Kimball, and Jon Dunn, 1981, *Birds of Southern California*, Los Angeles Audubon Society, Los Angeles, CA. An excellent reference covering status and distribution.

National Geographic Society, 1987, *Field Guide to the Birds of North America*, second edition, Washington, DC. The best of current field guides, but perhaps overwhelming to beginners.

Peterson, Roger Tory, 1961, *A Field Guide to Western Birds*, Houghton Mifflin, Boston, MA. A good guide for laypersons.

Terres, John K., 1980, *The Audubon Society Encyclopedia of North American Birds*, Alfred A. Knopf, New York, NY. A large book with a great amount of interesting, detailed information, written in non-technical language.

Index

183